HOUGHTON MIFFLIN

SOCIAL STUDIES

TENNESSEE

COMMUNITIES

Program Authors

Dr. Herman J. Viola
Dr. Sarah Witham Bednarz
Dr. Carlos E. Cortés

Dr. Cheryl Jennings
Dr. Mark C. Schug
Dr. Charles S. White

Visit **Education Place®**
www.eduplace.com/kids

 HOUGHTON MIFFLIN   BOSTON

Authors

Senior Author
Dr. Herman J. Viola
Curator Emeritus
Smithsonian Institution

Dr. Sarah Witham Bednarz
Associate Professor, Geography
Texas A&M University

Dr. Carlos E. Cortés
Professor Emeritus, History
University of California, Riverside

Dr. Cheryl Jennings
Project Director
Florida Institute of Education
University of North Florida

Dr. Mark C. Schug
Professor and Director
Center for Economic Education
University of Wisconsin, Milwaukee

Dr. Charles S. White
Associate Professor
School of Education
Boston University

Consulting Authors

Dr. Dolores Beltran
Assistant Professor
Curriculum Instruction
California State University, Los Angeles
(Support for English Language Learners)

Dr. MaryEllen Vogt
Co-Director
California State University Center for the
Advancement of Reading
(Reading in the Content Area)

Consultants

Philip J. Deloria
Associate Professor
Department of History and Program in
American Studies
University of Michigan

Lucien Ellington
UC Professor of Education and Asia Program
Co-Director
University of Tennessee, Chattanooga

Thelma Wills Foote
Associate Professor
University of California, Irvine

Stephen J. Fugita
Distinguished Professor
Psychology and Ethnic Studies
Santa Clara University

Charles C. Haynes
Senior Scholar
First Amendment Center

Ted Hemmingway
Professor of History
The Florida Agricultural & Mechanical
University

Douglas Monroy
Professor of History
Colorado College

Lynette K. Oshima
Assistant Professor
Department of Language, Literacy and
Sociocultural Studies and Social Studies
Program Coordinator
University of New Mexico

Jeffrey Strickland
Assistant Professor, History
University of Texas Pan American

Clifford E. Trafzer
Professor of History and American Indian
Studies
University of California, Riverside

Teacher Reviewers

Leah Dalrymple
J.E. Moss Elementary
Antioch, TN

Joy Eddings
Croft Middle School
Nashville, TN

Lee Farrar
McGavock Elementary School
Nashville, TN

Tracy Foxx
Lockeland Elementary
Nashville, TN

Amanda Griffin
Lawrenceburg Public School
Lawrenceburg, TN

Gina Hipsher
Joppa Elementary School
Rutledge, TN

Jeff Paulson
Thrasher Elementary School
Signal Mountain, TN

Betsy Potts
Goodlettsville Elementary School
Goodlettsville, TN

Brandi Self
Mooreland Heights Elementary
Knoxville, TN

Rebecca Verner
Social Studies Program Assistant Metro/
Nashville Public Schools
Nashville, TN

Ashley Witt
Blackman Elementary School
Murfreesboro, TN

Wes Wood
Thrasher Elementary School
Signal Mountain, TN

Printed in the U.S.A.

ISBN 10: 0-618-90624-X
ISBN 13: 978-0-618-90624-6

4 5 6 7 8 9-DOW-14 13 12 11 10 09 08

★★TENNESSEE★★

Curriculum Standards

1.0 CULTURE

Learning Expectations and Accomplishments

2.1.01 Understand the diversity of human cultures.

  a. Recognize most cultures preserve important personal and public items from the past.

  b. Recognize communities have customs and cultures that differ.

  c. Recognize patterns of cultural traits such as language, religion, and family structure.

2.1.02 Discuss cultures and human patterns of places and regions of the world.

  a. Identify diverse cultural groups within the communities of Tennessee.

  b. Compare and contrast the cultures of Tennessee's three grand divisions.

  c. Understand that Tennessee's culture has ties to other cultures in the world.

  d. Recognize that cultures have strong traditions of loyalty to their region or country.

  e. Compare the regional cultures of Tennessee to those of other states.

2.1.03 Recognize the contributions of individuals and people of various ethnic, racial, religious, and socioeconomic groups to the development of civilizations.

  a. Identify and explain the significance of selected stories, poems, statues, paintings, and other examples of local and state cultural heritage.

  b. Examine the effects of changing technologies on the local community and state.

  c. Recognize diverse cultural neighborhoods within Tennessee and America.

2.0 ECONOMICS

Learning Expectations and Accomplishments

2.2.01 Describe the potential costs and benefits of personal economic choices in a market economy.

  a. Explain how work provides income to purchase goods and services.

  b. Describe how society depends upon workers with specialized jobs and the ways in which they contribute to the production and exchange of goods and services.

2.2.02 Give examples of the interaction of individuals, businesses, and governments in a market economy.

  a. Give examples of the various institutions that make up economic systems such as families, workers, banks, labor unions, government agencies, small businesses, and large corporations.

  b. Recognize that communities around the state and world are economically interdependent.

  c. Know the major products of Tennessee.

2.2.03 Understand fundamental economic concepts.

  a. Categorize resources needed to operate industries.

  b. Understand the necessity of importing resources needed for industry.

3.0 GEOGRAPHY

Learning Expectations and Accomplishments

2.3.01 Understand how to use maps, globes, and other geographic representations, tools, and technologies to acquire, process and report information from a spatial perspective.

  a. Describe how the globe is a model of earth locating hemispheres, poles, and equator.

  b. Recognize that natural regions are represented on different types of maps by showing physical features, climate, vegetation, and natural resources.

c. Subdivide the world by positioning the equator, continents, oceans, and hemispheres on a map and globe.

d. Recognize that a map contains elements such as title, scale, symbols, legends, grids, cardinal and intermediate direction.

2.3.02 Recognize the interaction between human and physical systems around the world.

a. Analyze how individuals and populations depend upon land resources.

b. Describe the importance of physical geographic features on defining communities.

c. Understand the earth-sun relationship such as the varying length of day.

d. Understand the rudimentary elements to the hydrologic cycle.

e. List earth's natural resources such as minerals, air, water, and land.

2.3.03 Demonstrate how to identify and locate major physical and political features on globes and maps.

a. Show how landmasses and bodies of water are represented on maps and globes.

b. Locate the state of Tennessee and its major cities on a map.

c. Name the physical and human characteristics of the neighborhood and the community.

4.0 GOVERNANCE AND CIVICS

Learning Expectations and Accomplishments

2.4.01 Discuss the structure and purposes of governance.

a. Recognize how groups and organizations encourage unity and work with diversity to maintain order and security.

b. Identify functions of governments.

c. Be aware that every community has some form of governance.

d. Describe how governments establish order, provide security, and manage conflict.

2.4.02 Describe the Constitution of the United States and the Tennessee State Constitution in principle and practice.

a. Know that communities have different laws depending on the needs and problems of their community.

b. Recognize people who make laws and people who enforce them in Tennessee.

c. Identify ways that public officials are selected, including election and appointment.

d. Distinguish among local, state, and national government and identify representative leaders at these levels such as mayor, governor, and president.

2.4.03 Understand the rights, responsibilities, and privileges of citizens living in a democratic republic.

a. Identify characteristics of good citizenship such as establishing beliefs in justice, truth, equality, and responsibility for the common good.

b. Identify qualities of good citizenship.

c. Identify ordinary people who exemplify good citizenship.

2.4.04 Recognize the qualities of a contributing citizen in our participatory democracy.

a. Identify some governmental services in the community such as the libraries, schools, and parks, and explain their value to the community.

b. Explain how citizens fund various community services.

c. Explain the meaning of selected patriotic symbols and landmarks of Tennessee.

5.0 HISTORY

Learning Expectations and Accomplishments

2.5.01 Identify major events, people, and patterns in Tennessee, United States, and world history.

a. Explain the significance of various community, state, and national celebrations such as Memorial Day and Independence Day.

b. Explain how local people and events have influenced local community history.

2.5.02 Understand the place of historical events in the context of past, present and future.

a. Describe the order of events by using designation of time periods such as ancient times and modern times.

b. Use vocabulary related to chronology, including past, present and future.

c. Describe and measure calendar time by days, weeks, months, and years.

d. Comprehend that physical and human characteristics of communities change over time.

2.5.03 Explain how to use historical information acquired from a variety of sources.

- **a.** Identify and explain the significance of various community landmarks.
- **b.** Create and interpret timelines.
- **c.** Compare various interpretations of the same time period using evidence such as photographs and interviews.

6.0 INDIVIDUALS, GROUPS, AND INTERACTIONS

Learning Expectations and Accomplishments

2.6.01 Recognize the impact of individual and group decisions on citizens and communities.

- **a.** Describe how groups work independently and cooperatively to accomplish goals within a community.
- **b.** Recognize individuals can belong to groups but still have their own identity.
- **c.** Know how to share and give opinions in a group.

2.6.02 Understand how groups can cause change at the local, state, national, and world levels.

- **a.** Identify and describe ways family, groups, and community influence an individual's daily life and personal choices.
- **b.** Recognize individuals have a role in each group in which they participate.
- **c.** Recognize that each individual must make decisions about the work groups and play groups in which they participate.

Our Country's Culture

14

Vocabulary Preview
Reading Strategies: Predict/Infer, Summarize **16**

UNIT 2

People at Work 50

Vocabulary Preview
Reading Strategies: Question, Summarize 52

2.2.01a, 2.2.01b,
2.2.02a, 2.2.02b,
2.2.02c, 2.2.03a,
2.2.03b, 2.3.01d,
2.3.02a, 2.3.02e,
2.6.02b

UNIT 3

Our World

84

Vocabulary Preview
Reading Strategies: Question, Monitor/Clarify 86

2.1.03a, 2.3.01a,
2.3.01b, 2.3.01c,
2.3.01d, 2.3.02a,
2.3.02b, 2.3.02c,
2.3.02d, 2.3.02e,
2.3.03a, 2.3.03b,
2.3.03c, 2.6.02a

UNIT 4

Government

132

Vocabulary Preview

Reading Strategies: Summarize, Question 134

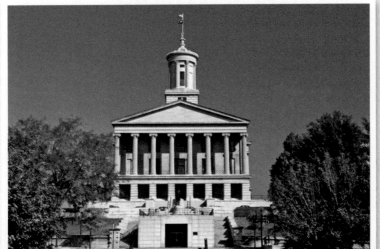

UNIT 5

In the Past

174

Vocabulary Preview
Reading Strategies: Predict/Infer, Monitor/Clarify **176**

2.1.03b, 2.4.03a,
2.4.03c, 2.5.01a,
2.5.01b, 2.5.02a,
2.5.02b, 2.5.02d,
2.5.03b, 2.5.03c,
2.6.01c

References

Resources

Extend Lessons

Connect to an important concept and dig into it. Extend your social studies knowledge!

Skill Lessons

Take a step-by-step approach to learning and practicing key social studies skills.

Visual Learning

Maps, graphs, and charts help you learn.

Maps

Charts and Graphs

Diagrams

Timelines

Fine Art

Constitution Day

Our country is a special place. One reason is because of the freedoms people have here. Citizens of the United States are free to say and print what they think, as long as the words do not hurt others. People are free to join groups. These freedoms are described in a paper called the United States Constitution.

The Constitution is a written plan that says what the nation's government can and cannot do. It was written more than 200 years ago by a group of leaders. They signed the Constitution on September 17, 1787. Today we celebrate Constitution Day and Citizenship Day during the week of September 17.

Activity

Make a Picture Dictionary The Constitution gives you many freedoms, such as freedom to speak and write, freedom to believe what you want, and freedom to meet with groups. Make a picture dictionary that shows the freedoms you have in the United States.

UNIT 1

Our Country's Culture

"The world's a lovely
Place to be
Because we are
A family."

—Mary Ann Hoberman, Poet

The Big Idea

What is part of a person's culture?

Vocabulary Preview

Technology

e • **glossary**
e • **word games**
www.eduplace.com/kids/hmss/

tradition

A **tradition** can be a holiday meal that families share every year. page 26

culture

Culture is the way of life of a group of people. Stories are a part of culture. page 19

Reading Strategy

Use the **predict and infer** reading strategy in Lessons 1 and 2 and the **summarize** strategy in Lessons 3 and 4.

country

A **country** is a part of the world with its own leaders and rules. The United States of America is our country. **page 34**

landmark

The Hermitage is a Tennessee landmark. A **landmark** is something that helps people know a place. **page 42**

Culture and Customs

Vocabulary

culture

custom

Reading Skill

Compare and Contrast

STANDARDS

CORE: 2.1.01c Cultural traits: language, religion, family **2.6.01b** Individual and group identity **2.6.02a** Families and groups influence daily life and choices **2.6.02b** Individuals have roles in different groups

Build on What You Know

You may be a student, a child, and a friend. These names describe who you are and what you do.

Groups

A group is a number of people who live together, work together, or spend time together. Your family is a group. Your school class is a group. You have a different job to do for every group you belong to.

main idea

A soccer team is a group. Each person in a group is different from all others.

Parts of Culture

The way of life of a group of people is called their **culture.** Clothes, food, music, and language are part of your culture. Your beliefs, or religion, are part of your culture. You learn about your culture from the people around you. You also learn about customs. A **custom** is something people usually do at a certain time.

Review What customs do you have in your family?

Some families have a custom of breaking a piñata at birthday parties.

Reading stories together at bedtime is a custom in some families.

You Learn From People

You learn about your culture from the people in the groups you belong to. They teach you about your culture and its customs. They teach you how to behave. Charan learns from these three groups:

main idea

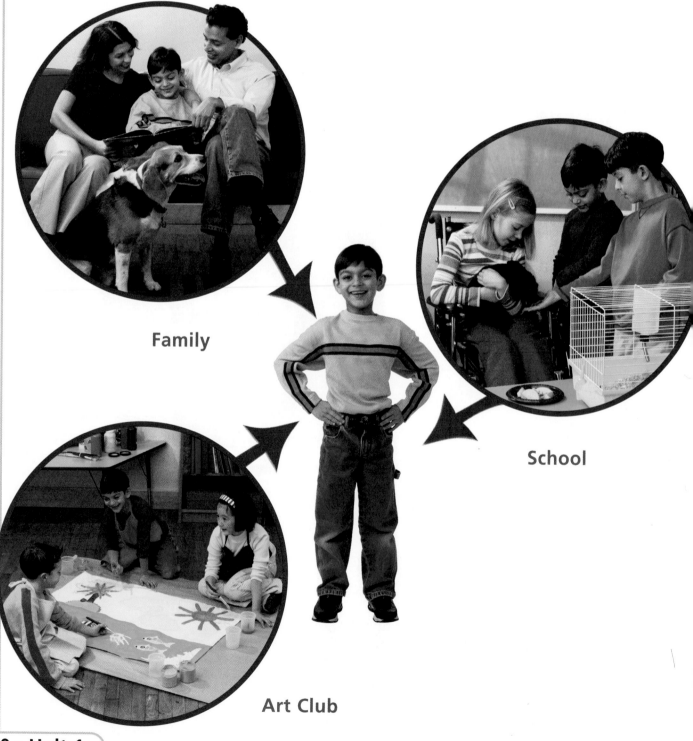

Family

School

Art Club

Making Choices

You learn how to behave from the people around you. You talk to people and watch how they act. You see the choices they make. Then it is up to you to decide how you will act and what you will do.

Review What groups help you learn what choices to make?

I learned to raise my hand when I want to speak in class.

Lesson Review

 1. 2.1.01c 2. 2.6.02a **Activity** 2.6.02a

❶ **Vocabulary** Write a sentence about the parts of **culture**.

❷ **Main Idea** What is one thing you can learn from people in the groups you belong to?

Activity Draw a picture to tell about a custom in your family or school.

Map and Globe Skills

Review: Maps and Globes

▶ **Vocabulary**

globe

map

A **globe** is a model of Earth. It shows that Earth is round like a ball. A **map** is a flat drawing of a place as seen from above. The title of the map tells you what the map shows. You can use a globe and a world map to find continents, oceans, and other places.

Learn the Skill

Step 1 Look at the globe. Oceans are usually colored blue on globes and maps.

Step 2 Find the Atlantic Ocean on the globe and on the world map. In what way is the ocean the same on the map and the globe?

Step 3 Continents are the big bodies of land you see on a globe and a world map. There are seven continents on Earth. Find a continent on the globe and the world map.

North Pole

South Pole

Practice the Skill

Look at the globe and the map. Then follow the directions.

1 What is the title of the map?

2 Compare the globe and the world map. Tell how they are alike and different.

3 Look at the globe and find the continent where you live. Then find it on the map. Write its name on a sheet of paper.

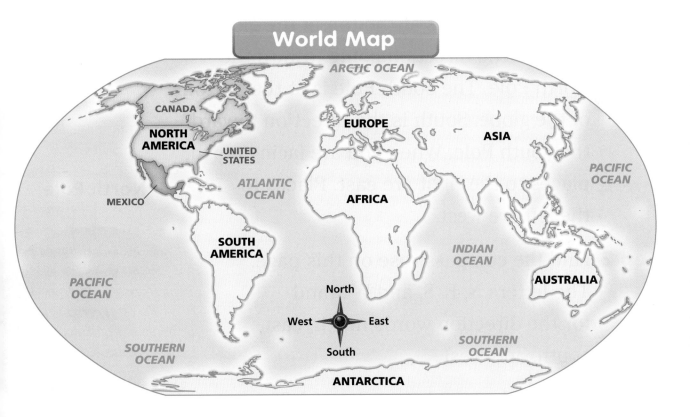

World Map

ARCTIC OCEAN

CANADA

NORTH AMERICA

EUROPE

ASIA

UNITED STATES

PACIFIC OCEAN

ATLANTIC OCEAN

MEXICO

AFRICA

SOUTH AMERICA

INDIAN OCEAN

PACIFIC OCEAN

AUSTRALIA

North

West — East

South

SOUTHERN OCEAN

SOUTHERN OCEAN

ANTARCTICA

23

Review: Symbols and Directions

▶ **Vocabulary**

compass rose
symbol

Directions help people find places on globes and maps. A **compass rose** shows directions.

Symbols are pictures that stand for real things. Most maps use symbols. A map key, or legend, explains what the symbols stand for.

Learn the Skill

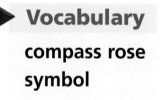

Step 1 The North Pole is at the top of the globe. North is the direction going toward the North Pole. The South Pole is at the bottom of the globe. South is the direction toward the South Pole. When you are facing north, places to the right are east. Places to the left are west.

Step 2 Find the compass rose on this page. The letters N, E, S, and W stand for the direction words north, east, south, and west.

North Pole

Step 3 Look at the map key, or legend. The symbol for forest is a tree. Find the symbol for forest on the map.

South Pole

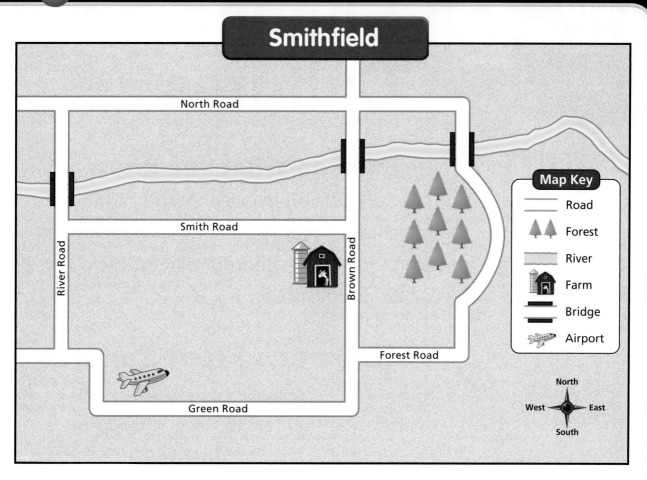

Smithfield

North Road

Smith Road

River Road

Brown Road

Forest Road

Green Road

Map Key

- Road
- Forest
- River
- Farm
- Bridge
- Airport

North
West — East
South

Practice the Skill

Look at the map. Then follow the directions.

1 Look at the map key, or legend. Describe the symbol for road.

2 Find the roads on the map.

3 Look at the river symbol on the map key. Find the river on the map. What is a symbol that touches the river?

4 Use the compass rose and map key to answer the question: What is west of the farm?

Sharing Cultures

Vocabulary

tradition
legend

Reading Skill

Main Idea and Details

STANDARDS
CORE: 2.1.01a Cultures preserve personal and public items
2.1.03a Local and state heritage: stories, poems, statues, paintings
EXTEND: 2.1.03a Local and state heritage: stories

Build on What You Know

Have you ever eaten food from another country? When people share things from different places, they share their cultures.

Traditions From Cultures

Families share their cultures by sharing their traditions. A **tradition** is an idea or custom that is passed down from one person to another. Traditions help people remember their cultures.

main idea

A tradition can be doing a paper-folding craft from Japan or eating turkey at Thanksgiving.

Remembering the Past

Traditions are one way that people can remember the past. Museums also show what life was like in the past. We can find out what was important to families by looking in museums. Some museums show things people used everyday, such as tools and dolls. Museums and libraries may also have important papers, books, paintings, and statues for everyone to see.

main idea

Review What is one way people remember things from the past?

CHILDREN OF APPALACHIA

You can see toys children played with in the past at the Museum of Appalachia in Norris, Tennessee.

Sharing Stories and Poems

People share their culture through stories. Some stories are called legends. A **legend** is a story that has been told for years and years. Some legends tell about a made-up person or animals that act like people. Others tell about a real person. Some legends about real people are not always true.

What do you think this girl is reading a legend about?

People also share their culture through poetry. William Porter Lawrence was from Nashville, Tennessee. He wrote the poem "Oh Tennessee, My Tennessee" while he was far from home. The poem describes the deep lakes, fine schools, and strong people of Tennessee. It became Tennessee's state poem.

Review What are two ways people can share cultures?

William Porter Lawrence wrote a poem about the culture of Tennessee.

Lesson Review
1. 2.1.01a 2. 2.1.03a **Activity** 2.1.01a, 2.1.03a

❶ **Vocabulary** Write a sentence about a **tradition** in your family.

❷ **Main Idea** Tell some ways that museums and libraries share culture from the past.

Activity Draw a picture of someone sharing his or her culture with you. Tell what you are learning. Then tell how you are learning it.

Davy Crockett and Raccoon

The story of Davy Crockett is a legend that is part of Tennessee's culture.

Davy Crockett was the best hunter in Tennessee. All the animals in the woods knew that if Davy shot, he never missed.

Furry Raccoon was high up in a tree one day. Raccoon saw Davy, and Davy saw her. Raccoon thought fast. Just as Davy raised his gun, she raised her paw. "Please, Sir, are you Davy Crockett, the best hunter in Tennessee?"

"Yes, I am," said Davy proudly.

"Please, Sir, would you be so kind? I always hoped to shake your hand."

"Sure. Come on down," Davy said.

Raccoon came down from the tree. She looked up at Davy and said, "Oh, Sir, you look so extra tall and strong from here!"

"That's nice to hear," Davy said. He put down his gun to shake her paw.

"You are very kind, Sir," said Raccoon. Slowly she backed away.

"You are kind yourself," said Davy.

"And you are very smart, Sir," said Raccoon. All at once she dashed away.

Davy laughed. "You are very smart yourself!" he called out after her.

"Thank you, Sir!" Raccoon called from very far away.

Activities

1. **Talk About It** Retell this story in your own words.

2. **Write About It** Write a story about another person from Tennessee.

Read a Calendar

▶ Vocabulary

calendar

Special days can help us remember traditions and events from the past. A calendar can help people keep track of the events. A **calendar** is a way of showing time. A calendar shows months, weeks, and days for one year.

Learn the Skill

Step 1 Name the months of the year in order. Start with January. Then look at the calendar page at right. What month does it show?

Step 2 Each row on the calendar shows one week. Name the seven days of the week. Start with Sunday.

Step 3 Every day of the month has a number, or date. Find the square with the number 6. The date of that day is November 6.

Step 4 Find the event on the first Saturday of the month. What is it?

Practice the Skill

Look at this town calendar page.
Then answer the questions.

1 How many days are in November?

2 Find the Fall Fair on the calendar. How many weeks later is Veterans Day?

NOVEMBER

Sunday	Monday	Tuesday	Wednesday	Thursday	Friday	Saturday
			1	2	3	4 Fall Fair
5	6	7 Election Day	8	9	10	11 Veterans Day
12	13	14	15	16	17	18
19	20	21	22	23 Thanksgiving	24	25
26	27	28	29	30		

Many Cultures, One Country

Vocabulary

country
immigrant
community

Reading Skill

Draw Conclusions

STANDARDS
CORE: 2.1.01b Communities have different customs and cultures **2.1.02e** Compare regional cultures of Tennessee to other states **2.1.03c** Diverse cultural neighborhoods in Tennessee and America
EXTEND: 2.1.02a Diverse cultural groups in Tennessee **2.1.02c** Tennessee's culture related to world cultures

Build on What You Know

Moving to a new place can mean many changes. What can a family do to remember the place they came from?

United States Cultures

The United States is our country. A **country** is a part of the world with its own leaders and rules. Our country has many cultures. Many immigrants come to live in our country. An **immigrant** is a person who moves from one country to another.

main idea

Our Country, The United States of America

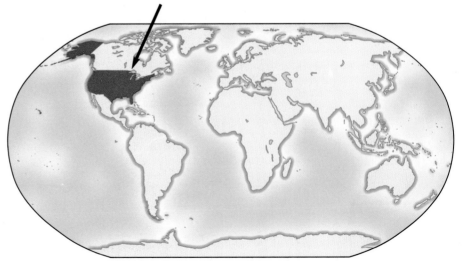

Communities and Cultures

Immigrants bring their cultures to the United States. Their cultures might include traditions such as a special dance or food. Immigrants share their traditions and customs with each community they join. A **community** is a place where people live, play, and work together. Sometimes, different neighborhoods within a community have different cultures. A neighborhood is a part of a community or town.

Review What is one tradition in your community?

Chinese New Years parade in San Francisco

Italian street fair in New York City

Tennessee Traditions

Tennessee has many communities that have their own customs and traditions. For example, Knoxville has a Kuumba Festival each year. During the festival, African American artists show their artwork. The Tennessee communities of Gatlinburg and Arlington both have big Independence Day parades. Gatlinburg holds its famous parade at midnight each year. Arlington's parade has a contest for wagons and decorated bikes.

These men play traditional African music at Knoxville's Kuumba Festival.

Shared Cultures

Some Tennessee communities 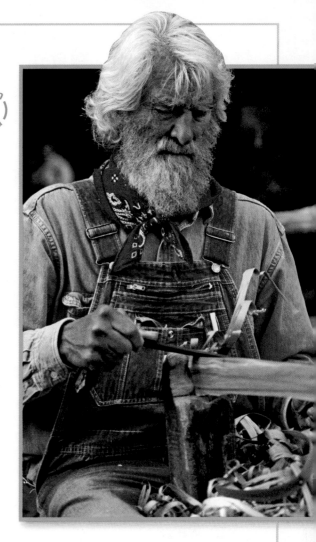 share their cultures and traditions with communities outside Tennessee. People in eastern Tennessee share wood carving, square dances, and games such as marbles with people who live nearby in Virginia and North Carolina.

main idea

Wood carving is part of East Tennessee's culture.

Review What are two traditions that people in eastern Tennessee share with other states?

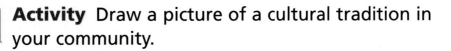

Lesson Review

1. 2.1.01b, 2.1.03c 2. 2.1.02e **Activity** 2.1.01b, 2.1.03c

❶ **Vocabulary** Tell something about the United States using the word **immigrant.**

❷ **Main Idea** Does every community in Tennessee have the same customs and traditions? Tell why you answered yes or no.

HANDS ON

Activity Draw a picture of a cultural tradition in your community.

Celebrate TENNESSEE!

Every year fairs and festivals take place in many Tennessee communities. Sometimes different neighborhoods within one city have festivals. Each festival celebrates different people and different cultures. These festivals all celebrate the many cultures in Tennessee in fun ways.

The Beale Street Zydeco Festival in Memphis celebrates music from French and Caribbean culture.

People learn about Choctaw customs at Memphis's Choctaw Heritage Festival.

The Uncle Dave Macon
Days Festival celebrates
Appalachian culture.

Activities

1. **Talk About It** Talk about
   the fairs and festivals in your
   community. What cultures do
   they celebrate?

2. **Create It** Create a poster
   for one of the festivals on
   these pages.

Tennessee's Heritage

People in Tennessee live in different divisions, but they are all Tennesseans. Tennessee has its own heritage and culture. **Heritage** is all the important traditions that are passed down in families and communities. You can learn about Tennessee's heritage by reading books, listening to music, or visiting a Tennessee landmark. A **landmark** is a place or thing that is special to a community.

main idea ★

This statue helps people remember Davy Crockett.

Graceland is an important Memphis landmark. It was once the home of Elvis Presley.

ERECTED BY GIFT OF
THE PEOPLE AND
THE LEGISLATURE
OF TENNESSEE,
TO THE MEMORY OF
COL. DAVID CROCKETT
BORN IN EAST TENNESSEE
AUG. 17TH, 1786,
AND GAVE HIS LIFE FOR
TEXAS LIBERTY AMID
THE SMOKING WALLS
OF THE "ALAMO"
SUNDAY MORNING
MARCH 6TH, 1836,

The Hermitage is a Tennessee landmark near Nashville. It was the home of Andrew Jackson. He was an important leader for Tennessee and the United States. The Hermitage is part of your state heritage.

Review What Tennessee landmarks have you seen?

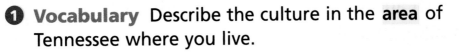

Lesson Review

1. 2.1.02a 2. 2.1.02b, 2.1.02d **Activity** 2.1.03a

1 Vocabulary Describe the culture in the **area** of Tennessee where you live.

2 Main Idea How is the culture in your grand division different from the culture in another grand division?

Activity Draw a picture of a landmark in Tennessee that you know. Tell what the landmark is showing.

Cardinal and Intermediate Directions

▶ **Vocabulary**

cardinal
directions
intermediate
directions

When people travel from one place to another, they often use maps to find their way. A compass rose shows them the directions. The **cardinal directions** are north, south, east, and west. But there are **intermediate directions** too. Those fall between cardinal directions.

Learn the Skill

Look at the compass rose below.

Step 1 Find the cardinal directions north, south, east, and west.

Step 2 Find the line halfway between north and east. This line points in the intermediate direction called **northeast**.

Step 3 Now find the line halfway between south and west. Which intermediate direction is it?

Step 4 Find the letters NE, SE, SW, and NW. These letters stand for the intermediate direction words **northeast**, **southeast**, **southwest**, and **northwest**.

Practice the Skill

Look at the map. Then follow the directions.

1. Find Gettysburg, Pennsylvania. In what direction do you go to get to Selma, Alabama?

2. Find Jackson, Tennessee. What direction do you go to get to Lincoln, Nebraska?

3. Leave Reno, Nevada, and travel northeast. Which city on this map do you reach first?

United States

Big Ideas

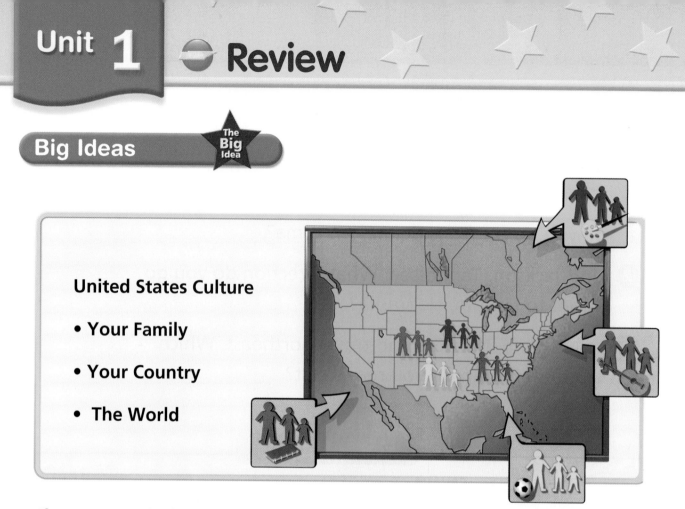

United States Culture

• Your Family

• Your Country

• The World

Choose words from the unit that help describe the picture.

1. You learn about your culture from your _____. 2.6.02a

2. Languages, music, and games are part of _____. 2.1.01c

3. Immigrants from around the _____ bring their cultures to the United States. 2.1.02c

4. There is a different culture in each of Tennessee's three _____. 2.1.02.b

5. Tennessee communities have their own customs and _____. 2.1.02a

Vocabulary

Choose the letter of the word to match the correct definition.

6. A story that has been passed down for a long time 2.1.03a

7. An idea or custom passed down from one person to another 2.1.01a

8. The way of life of a group of people 2.1.01c

9. A building or monument that helps people know a place 2.1.01a

A. **culture** (page 19)

B. **landmark** (page 42)

C. **legend** (page 28)

D. **immigrant** (page 34)

E. **tradition** (page 26)

Critical Thinking

10. Name a landmark in Tennessee. Tell why it is important to Tennessee's culture. 2.1.01a, 2.1.03a

11. What languages might people in the United States speak? Tell why many languages are spoken in this country. 2.1.01c

12. In the legend, *Davy Crockett and Raccoon*, the Raccoon fools Davy. What else could Davy have said to Raccoon? 2.1.03a

Unit Project

The Big Idea

Culture Banner

Use pictures to make a Tennessee culture banner that shows the people and symbols that make up Tennessee's many cultures.

1 Draw or bring in pictures to put on the banner.

2 Write a title and your name on the banner.

3 Arrange the pictures on your banner.

2.1.02a

CURRENT EVENTS
WEEKLY (WR) READER

Current Events Project

What traditions and celebrations take place in your community? Make an exhibit about **Celebrations in the News.**

2.1.02a

Technology

Read articles about current events at www.eduplace.com/kids/hmss/

Read A Calendar

Directions

Use the calendar to do Numbers 13 and 14.

13 Which holiday is on October 23? 2.5.02c
  Ⓐ Columbus Day
  Ⓑ Christmas
  Ⓒ Thanksgiving
  Ⓓ United Nations Day

14 Which of these **best** describes what this calendar page
  shows? 2.5.02c
  Ⓐ days and weeks
  Ⓑ days, weeks, month
  Ⓒ minutes and days
  Ⓓ weeks and months

People at Work

"At Dudley Market
now I tell
Most kinds of articles
they sell:
Hats, caps and bonnets blue
And trousers wide
enough for two"

—Ben Boucher, Poet

The Big Idea

What are some ways people earn and spend money?

Unit 2 People at Work

Vocabulary Preview

 **Technology**
e • glossary
e • word games
www.eduplace.com/kids/hmss/

income

The money people earn when they work is their **income.** Sam's income is the $5.00 he earns each week on his paper route.

page 54

producer

A **producer** is someone who provides a service or makes goods. Julie has a dogwalking service, so she is a producer.

page 60

Reading Strategy

Use the **question** reading strategy in Lessons 1 and 2 and the **summarize** strategy in Lessons 3 and 4.

industry

An **industry** is a group of businesses that produce or make something. A guitar factory is part of the music industry. **page 68**

trade

Trade is the buying and selling of goods and services. You trade money for lemonade at a drink stand. **page 73**

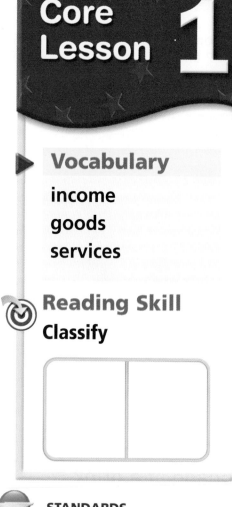

Core Lesson 1

Vocabulary
income
goods
services

Reading Skill
Classify

STANDARDS
CORE: 2.2.01a Work provides
income; goods and services

Work

Build on What You Know

What kinds of work do the adults you know do? What jobs have you done to earn money?

Ways to Earn Money

When people work, they usually earn money. This money is their **income.** People do different kinds of work to earn an income. One person may earn income from selling paintings that he made. Another person may earn income by selling a crop she grew.

main
(★)
idea

I own a small business. I like to help people with computer problems. I also like being my own boss!

Sometimes people sell their skills or their time. They are paid for teaching in a school or working in a shop.

Mechanics use their skills to repair cars and other machines.

Some tour guides teach people about what life was like long ago.

Review What work do people do to earn income?

Goods

Some people earn income by making or selling goods. **Goods** are the things people make or grow. Cotton, corn, and soybeans are goods. Tools, cars, and sneakers are goods too.

Workers at this Spring Hill, Tennessee factory make cars. Cars and trucks are goods.

Services

Some people earn income by providing services. **Services** are things that people do to help other people.  Doctors, teachers, and dog walkers provide services. Workers and families use their income to buy goods and services they need and want.

Review What is one way that goods and services are different?

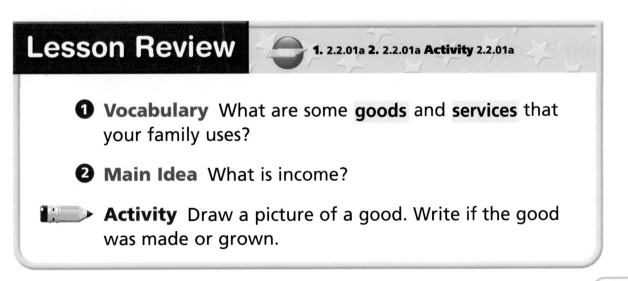

Lesson Review
1. 2.2.01a 2. 2.2.01a **Activity** 2.2.01a

❶ **Vocabulary** What are some **goods** and **services** that your family uses?

❷ **Main Idea** What is income?

Activity Draw a picture of a good. Write if the good was made or grown.

Read a Bar Graph

Many people earn income making, growing, or selling food. This bar graph shows how much milk cows in the United States produce each year.

▶ **Vocabulary**

bar graph

Learn the Skill

Using a **bar graph** is a way to compare things. The bars show how much there is of something.

Step 1 The numbers and words at the side of the graph tell how much milk. On this graph, the number 30 stands for 30 billion pounds of milk.

Step 2 Along the bottom of the graph are the names of some places where milk is produced.

Step 3 Look at the bar above California. It goes up to 30. That means that in California, cows produce 30 billion pounds of milk each year. How much milk do cows in Wisconsin produce?

Practice the Skill

Look at the graph below. Then answer the questions.

1 How much milk is produced in New York each year?

2 Which bar on the graph shows the smallest amount of milk produced?

3 Where do cows produce more milk each year, Wisconsin or New York?

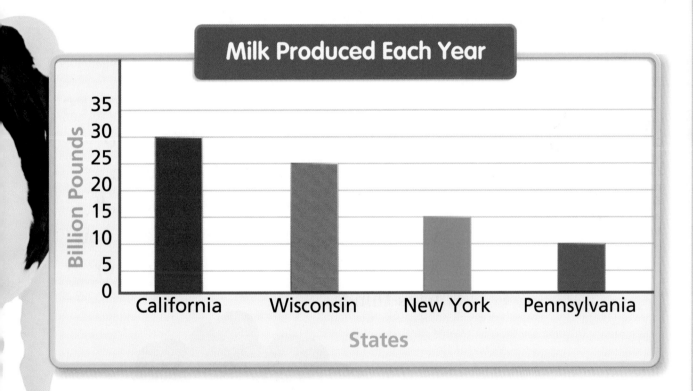

Milk Produced Each Year

Depending on One Another

Build on What You Know

Do you make the things you need and want? Do you buy some things? You depend on other people for things you want and need.

Producers and Consumers

Do you grow your own apples to eat? If so, then you are a producer. A **producer** makes or grows goods. If you buy your apples from a store, you are a consumer. A **consumer** buys or uses things.

People can be producers and consumers. They depend on each other to get what they need. When you buy things such as lemons and sugar to make lemonade, you are a consumer. When you sell the lemonade you made, you are a producer.

Review When have you been a consumer?

I am a producer. I make lemonade and sell it.

I am a consumer. I buy the lemonade and drink it. Yummy!

LEMONADE 25¢

Depending on Each Other

Look at the chart to see how consumers and producers depend on each other. The Jones family lives in Clarksville, Tennessee. They depend on people and businesses in Clarksville for the goods and services they need and want.

The Jones family buys the food they need from the grocery store. They depend on the store to get goods.

The grocery store owner depends on people like the Jones family to buy his goods. He uses his income to keep the store full of food and to buy the goods and services he needs.

The people and businesses in Clarksville also depend on the Jones family. Businesses need consumers to buy their goods and services.

Review In what ways do you depend on the businesses in your town?

Families like the Jones family and businesses like the grocery store depend on banks. Banks can keep income safe and loan people money when they need it.

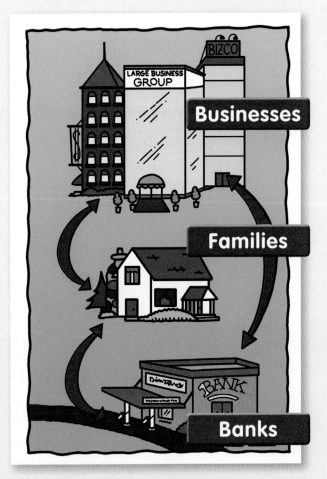

Big businesses depend on people to buy their goods and services. They also depend on banks to protect their money.

Specialized Workers

We depend on specialized workers to make and sell different goods and services. A **specialized worker** is a person who does just one main job. Farmers are specialized workers. A soybean farmer in Tennessee specializes in growing soybeans. The farmer may sell his soybeans for feed. He may also sell it to a company.

This farmer may sell his soybeans to a company that makes crayons out of soybeans.

The company uses the soybeans to make goods.
Then the company sells those goods to people
around the world.

Crayons made from soybeans

Review What does a specialized worker do?

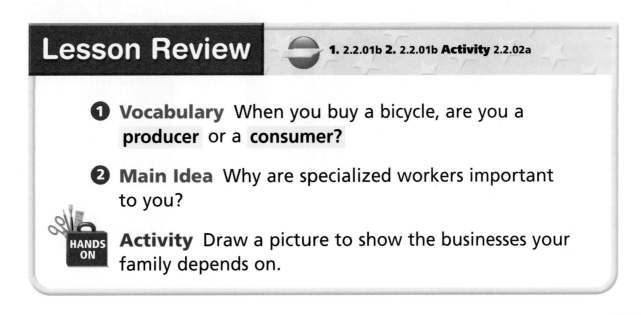

Lesson Review
1. 2.2.01b 2. 2.2.01b **Activity** 2.2.02a

❶ **Vocabulary** When you buy a bicycle, are you a **producer** or a **consumer?**

❷ **Main Idea** Why are specialized workers important to you?

HANDS ON **Activity** Draw a picture to show the businesses your family depends on.

Mesopotamia

First Farmers

Were people always producers of their food? More than ten thousand years ago, people did not live in cities and towns or on farms. Instead, they moved from place to place.

Each person in the group had a job to do. Some people made tools to use. Others took seeds and planted them in soil. The plants grew well. People picked the grain. They used some of it and saved the rest for planting.

Some of the first farmers lived in Mesopotamia.

2. Planting seeds

Farmers began to live near their fields so they could care for their plants. Small towns grew up nearby.

1. Making tools

First farmers needed tools to plant seeds and cut grain.

The drawing below shows the specialized jobs of some first farmers.

4. Grinding grain
Farmers ground grain into flour.

5. Baking bread
Flour was made into bread.

3. Harvesting grain
Farmers cut the grain. Some was stored away.

Activities

1. **Chart It** Make a flow chart that shows the steps described on these pages.

2. **Think About It** In what ways were the first farmers like farmers today?

Resources and Products

Build on What You Know

Look at your desk. What is it made out of? Where do producers get the materials they need to make goods?

Resources for Industry

Logging is an important industry in Tennessee. An **industry** is a kind of business that produces or makes something. Industries need three kinds of resources to make goods.

main idea (★)

The logging industry sells trees it cuts down to make paper.

A **natural resource** is something from nature that can be used by people. Logging companies use natural resources such as soil, water, and trees. They grow forests for lumber. A **human resource** is a person who works to produce goods or services. Loggers are human resources. They cut down the trees. **Capital resources** are things that are used to make and move other goods. A truck is a capital resource.

Review What resources does the logging industry need?

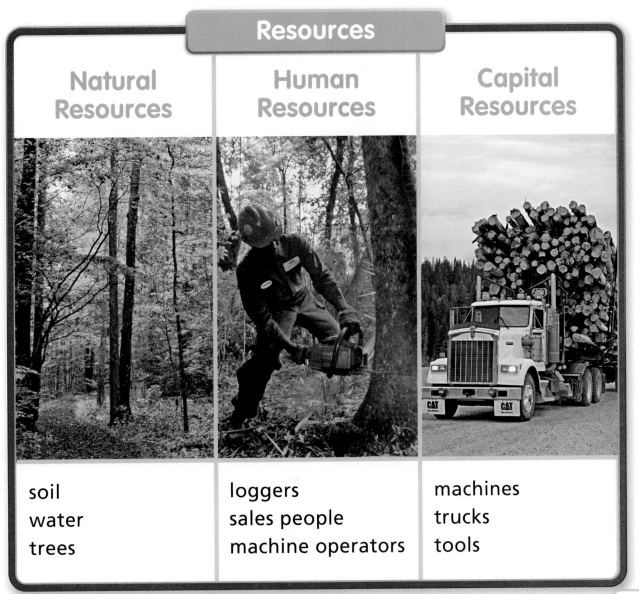

Resources		
Natural Resources	**Human Resources**	**Capital Resources**
soil	loggers	machines
water	sales people	trucks
trees	machine operators	tools

Tennessee Products and Industry

Many industries make products in Tennessee. A product is a good. Cars, clothing, and toys are products. Some products are made by important industries in Tennessee. Two big auto companies build cars in Tennessee. Other factories make car parts. They are all part of the auto industry.

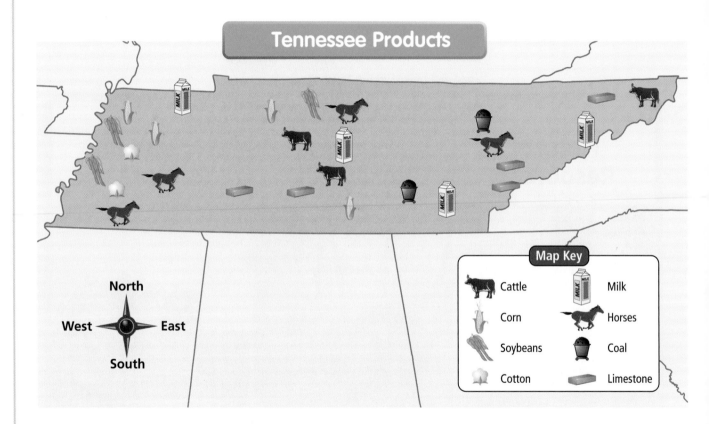

Tennessee Products

North
West — East
South

Map Key

Cattle		Milk	
Corn		Horses	
Soybeans		Coal	
Cotton		Limestone	

Mining is another important industry in Tennessee.
There are coal, limestone and zinc mines in Tennessee.

Review What are some industries in Tennessee?

Lesson Review

1. 2.2.02c 2. 2.3.02a **Activity** 2.2.03a

❶ **Vocabulary** Write or say a sentence about an **industry** in Tennessee.

❷ **Main Idea** Explain how industries depend on natural resources.

HANDS ON **Activity** Draw a picture of a product being made. Point out the natural, human, and capital resources being used to make it.

People and Nations Trade

Build on What You Know

Trading toys is one way to get what you want. What do businesses do to get things to make goods?

Barter

When you exchange a toy for a baseball card, you barter. **Barter** takes place when people exchange goods or services without using money. Long ago, barter was the way most people got the things they wanted and needed.

I'll give you this pig for two pounds of beets.

I'll trade one pound of beets for your pig.

Trade

Many times, barter does not work well. That is why people today usually pay for goods and services with money. Whether you barter or use money, you are taking part in trade. **Trade** is the buying and selling of goods and services. You take part in trade when you buy an apple.

main idea (★)

Review What is one way you could take part in trade?

Skill **Visual Learning** What do people use to help them trade goods?

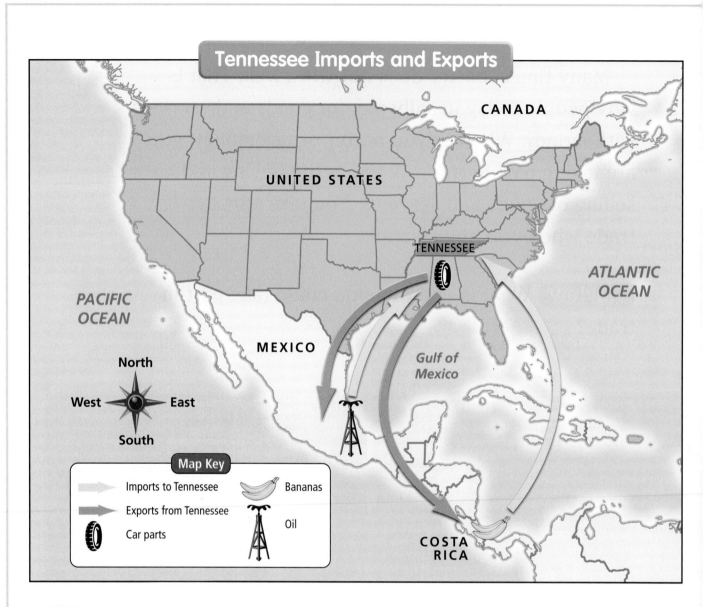

Tennessee Imports and Exports

CANADA

UNITED STATES

TENNESSEE

ATLANTIC OCEAN

PACIFIC OCEAN

MEXICO

Gulf of Mexico

North

West — East

South

COSTA RICA

Map Key

→ Imports to Tennessee

→ Exports from Tennessee

Car parts

Bananas

Oil

Skill **Reading Maps** Which arrows are symbols for imports?

Imports and Exports

People, communities, and countries all trade with each other to get the resources or products they need for industry. People export the resources they have enough of. **Export** means to send things *to* another country. Countries import the resources they need. **Import** means to bring things *into* a country from another country.

*main
(★)
idea*

Using Tennessee Resources

Tennessee has natural resources like coal and aluminum. Tennessee exports these resources. Tennessee needs imported resources like oil for industry. People in Tennessee and around the world import and export goods and services.

(★) main idea

Oil tankers bring oil to the United States.

Tennessee exports cars like this.

Review What are the two ways countries trade with each other?

Lesson Review

1. 2.2.02b 2. 2.2.02b, 2.2.03b **Activity** 2.2.02b

❶ **Vocabulary** The buying and selling of goods and services is called _____.

❷ **Main Idea** What is one reason that countries trade with one another?

Activity Write about a time you bought or sold something. Tell how you take part in trade.

Economics

Money Around the World

People around the world use money to buy and sell things. They use money to buy food at stores. Owners of stores use money to buy more goods to sell. They buy goods from other states and countries too.

Every country decides what kind of money to use. The United States uses the dollar. Japan uses the yen. Learn other money names.

The European Union

euro

euro cent

Brazil

real

centavo

Kenya

shilling

cent

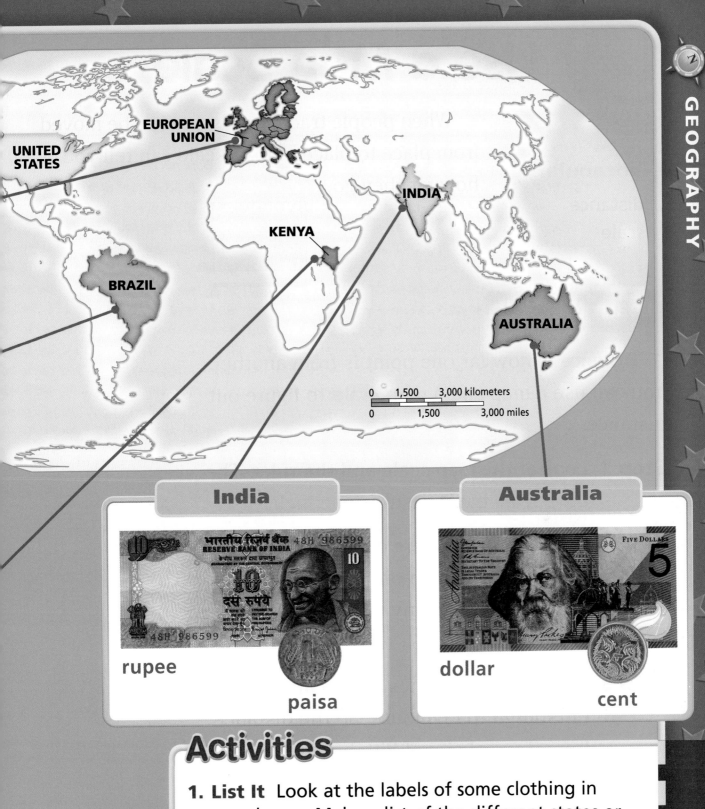

EUROPEAN UNION

UNITED STATES

INDIA

KENYA

BRAZIL

AUSTRALIA

0   1,500   3,000 kilometers
0   1,500   3,000 miles

India

rupee

paisa

Australia

dollar

cent

Activities

1. **List It** Look at the labels of some clothing in your home. Make a list of the different states or countries that you find on the labels.

2. **Make It** Use paper to make your own coin or paper money. Choose a name for your money.

Use a Map Scale

When people trade, goods need to be moved from place to place. A map scale can tell you how far they go.

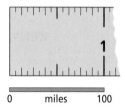

▶ **Vocabulary**

distance
scale

Learn the Skill

Distance is how far one point is from another. You can use a map and a map **scale** to figure out distance.

Step 1 Look at the map scale and the ruler. The blue scale bar measures one inch.

Step 2 Look at the numbers on the scale. They show that one inch on the map stands for 100 miles. How many miles do two inches stand for?

Step 3 It is about five inches on the map from Pittsburgh to Plymouth. So the distance from the real city of Pittsburgh to Plymouth must be about 500 miles.

Practice the Skill

**Look at the map. Follow the directions to find
distances. Use a ruler.**

1 About how many inches is it on the map from
Plymouth to Washington, D.C.?

2 How many miles is it from Plymouth to Washington,
D.C.? Use the scale to find out.

3 A truck carries clams from Plymouth to Ithaca. How
many miles does the truck travel?

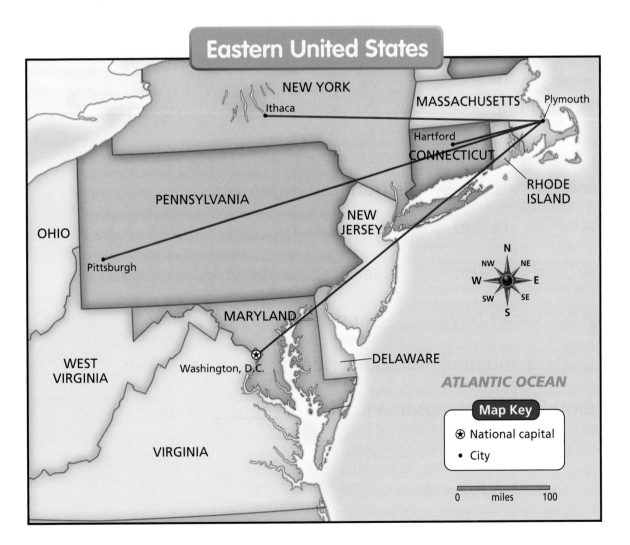

Eastern United States

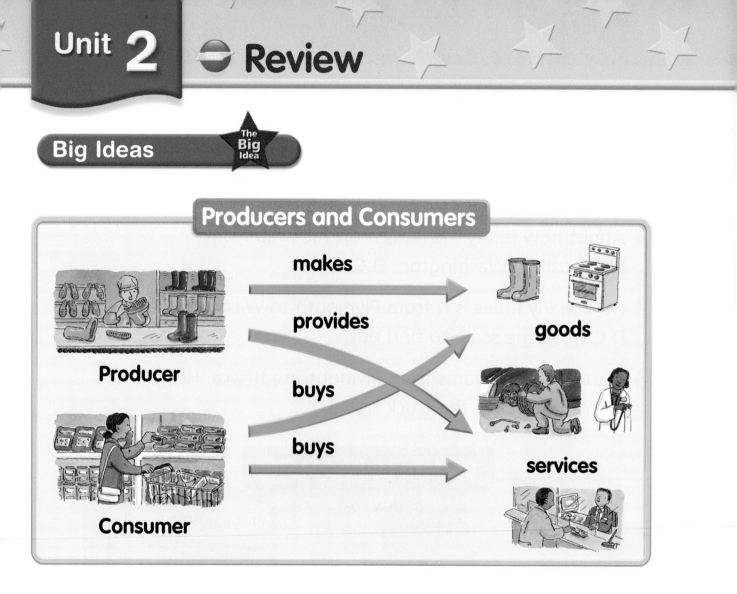

Producers and Consumers

Choose the missing words from the organizer.

1. A _____ makes goods. 2.2.01b, 2.2.02a

2. A producer also _____ services. 2.2.01b, 2.2.02a

3. A consumer buys _____ and services. 2.2.01a, 2.2.02a

4. Doctors and bank tellers provide _____. 2.2.01b, 2.2.02b

5. Clothing and things in a home are _____. 2.2.01b

Vocabulary

Use words from the box to complete the sentences.

6. Consumers earn _____ to pay for the things they want and need. **2.2.01a**

7. Industries need _____ and _____ to make goods. **2.2.03a**

8. Producers sell _____ and _____ to people. **2.2.02a**

9. _____ do only one main job. **2.2.01b**

> A. **natural resources**
> (page 69)
>
> B. **income** (page 54)
>
> C. **trade** (page 73)
>
> D. **services** (page 57)
>
> E. **specialized workers**
> (page 64)
>
> F. **human resources**
> (page 69)
>
> G. **goods** (page 56)

Critical Thinking

10. What are two examples of human resources? **2.2.03a**

11. Why do countries trade goods and services? **2.2.02b**

12. What are two ways people earn income? **2.2.01a**

Unit Project

The Big Idea

Make a Mobile

What goods and services did your family buy this week?

1 Write and draw some goods and services your family bought.

2 Choose three of your drawings.

3 Hang your family's purchases up to make a mobile.

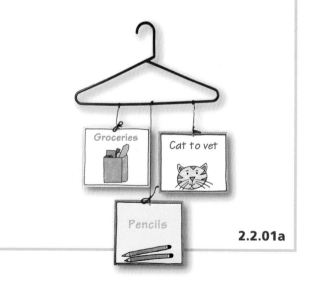

2.2.01a

CURRENT EVENTS
WEEKLY (WR) READER

Current Events Project

Find articles about jobs around the world. Publish a **Class Newspaper** about people at work around the world.

JOBS AROUND THE WORLD

Rug weaving   Fishing

2.2.01b

Technology

Read articles about current events at www.eduplace.com/kids/hmss/

Read a bar graph

Directions

Use the bar graph and what you know to do Numbers 13 and 14.

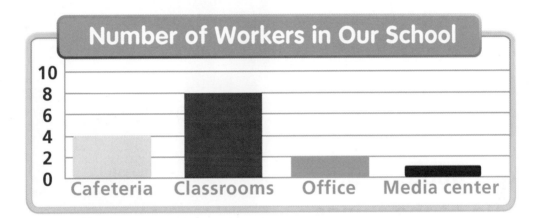

13 Which place at school has the **fewest** workers?   2.2.01b

Ⓐ Cafeteria

Ⓑ Classrooms

Ⓒ Office

Ⓓ Media center

14 Which bar shows the most workers in the school?   2.2.01b

Ⓐ purple

Ⓑ dark green

Ⓒ light green

Ⓓ red

UNIT 3

Our World

❝Look about you.
Take hold of the things
that are here.❞

—George Washington Carver

The Big Idea

What do you know
about Earth and
its people?

Unit 3

Our World

Vocabulary Preview

Technology
e • **glossary**
e • **word games**
www.eduplace.com/kids/hmss/

urban area

An **urban area** is a place where many people live and work closely together. page 98

continent

The United States is on the continent of North America. A **continent** is a large body of land. page 90

Reading Strategy

Use the **question** reading strategy in Lessons 1, 2, and 3 and the **monitor and clarify** strategy in Lessons 4, 5 and 6.

barrier

A **barrier** is something that separates two places. Mountains are one kind of land barrier. **page 108**

climate

Climate is the usual weather of a place over a long time. People in a cold climate need warm homes to live in. **page 123**

Your Address

Build on What You Know

What is the name of your community? Do you know the rest of your address?

States in a Country

Carlos is going to mail a letter to his cousin Len. Len lives on Green Street in the city of Chattanooga. Look at the envelope to see the rest of Len's address. What is Tennessee? What does U.S.A. mean?

STANDARDS
CORE: 2.3.03a Landmasses and bodies of water on maps and globes **2.3.03b** Locate Tennessee and its cities on maps
EXTEND: 2.3.01c Subdivide world on map

return address

stamp

address

Carlos Rivera
95 Rock Street
Memphis, Tennessee
37501

Len Ruis
27 Green Street
Chattanooga, Tennessee
37401
U.S.A.

Carlos

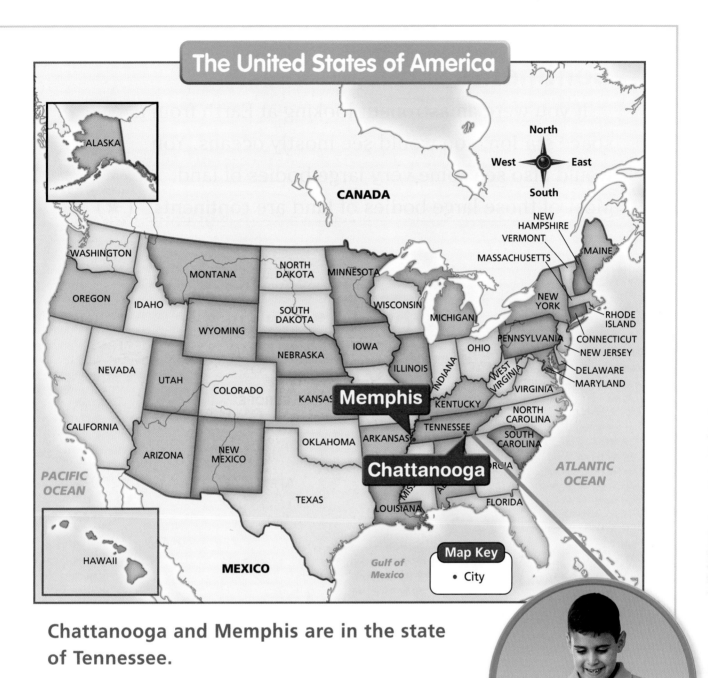

The United States of America

ALASKA

CANADA

North
West — East
South

WASHINGTON
OREGON
IDAHO
MONTANA
NORTH DAKOTA
MINNESOTA
WISCONSIN
MICHIGAN
NEW HAMPSHIRE
VERMONT
MASSACHUSETTS
MAINE
NEW YORK
RHODE ISLAND
SOUTH DAKOTA
WYOMING
IOWA
OHIO
PENNSYLVANIA
CONNECTICUT
NEW JERSEY
NEBRASKA
ILLINOIS
INDIANA
WEST VIRGINIA
DELAWARE
MARYLAND
NEVADA
UTAH
COLORADO
KANSAS
Memphis
KENTUCKY
VIRGINIA
CALIFORNIA
OKLAHOMA
ARKANSAS
TENNESSEE
NORTH CAROLINA
SOUTH CAROLINA
ARIZONA
NEW MEXICO
Chattanooga
ORGIA
PACIFIC OCEAN
TEXAS
MISS
A
FLORIDA
LOUISIANA
ATLANTIC OCEAN
HAWAII
MEXICO
Gulf of Mexico

Map Key
• City

Chattanooga and Memphis are in the state of Tennessee.

The letters U.S.A. on the envelope stand for the country of the United States of America. You learned that a country is a land that has the same laws and leaders. Tennessee is a state in the United States. A **state** is a part of a country. The United States is a country made up of 50 states.

Len

main
(★)
idea

Review What other states do you know?

89

Continents

If you were an astronaut looking at Earth from a space station, you would see mostly oceans. You would also see some very large bodies of land. Most of those large bodies of land are **continents.** (★) main idea

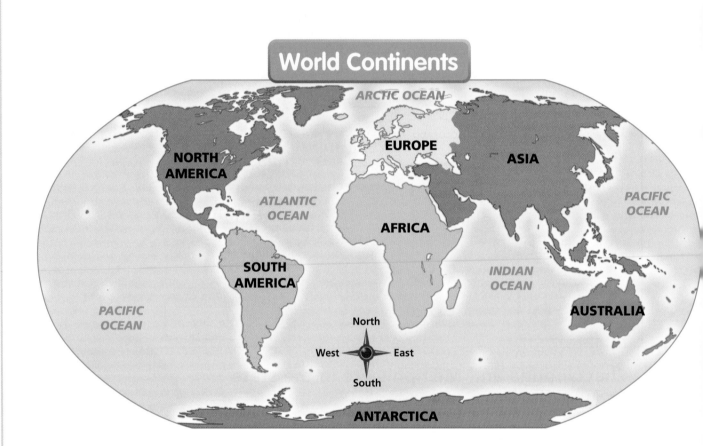

World Continents

Skill **Reading Maps** Find and name the seven continents on the map. Find and name the four oceans.

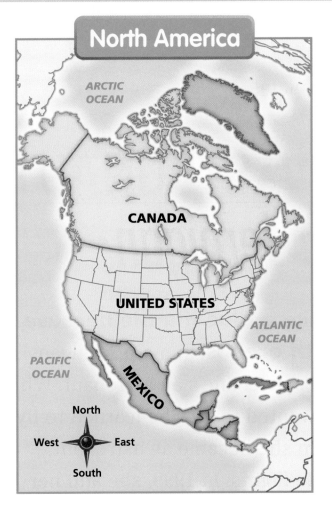

North America

ARCTIC OCEAN

CANADA

UNITED STATES

PACIFIC OCEAN

ATLANTIC OCEAN

MEXICO

North
West · East
South

The United States is on the continent of North America. The United States shares North America with two other large countries. They are Canada and Mexico. Seven small nations and many island countries are part of North America too. **Nation** is another word for country.

main idea

Which oceans touch North America?

Review What is one way that Mexico and the United States are alike?

Lesson Review

1. 2.3.03b 2. 2.3.03a **Activity** 2.3.03b

❶ Vocabulary Write a sentence that tells where Tennessee is. Use the words **nation, state,** and **continent** in the sentence.

❷ Main Idea What are Earth's seven continents?

Activity Look at pages R12–R13. Write about the location of your city compared to one city on the map.

Tennessee Astronaut:
Tamara E. Jernigan

From space, Earth looks like a blue marble because most of Earth is covered with oceans. Tamara Jernigan knows just how Earth looks from space. She's an astronaut. When she was young, Jernigan always wanted to fly. She learned to fly airplanes when she grew up. Then she became an astronaut. Jernigan flew on five space shuttle flights. In 1999, she and her crew were the first to land at the International Space Station.

"It is interesting to think that everyone you know lives on that big, blue marble."

—Tamara Jernigan

Activities

1. **Talk About It** What do you think other colors in this photograph of Earth show?

2. **Draw It** Look at a map of the world. Then make your own map. Color and label the continents and oceans.

93

Map and Globe Skills

Parts of a Globe

To show locations on a globe, we use the **poles,** the **equator,** and the **hemispheres.**

▶ **Vocabulary**

pole
equator
hemisphere

Learn the Skill

The North and South poles are imaginary. You cannot see them on Earth, only on a globe.

Step 1 The Equator is an imaginary line around the middle of Earth. It is halfway between the North Pole and the South Pole.

Step 2 The Equator divides Earth into the Northern Hemisphere and the Southern Hemisphere.

Step 3 The maps on page 95 show that Earth may also be divided into Eastern and Western Hemispheres.

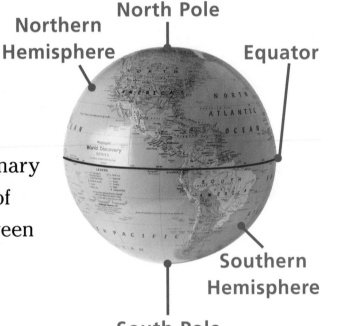

Practice the Skill

Look at the maps. Then follow the directions.

1 Find the continent where you live. Tell which hemispheres you live in.

2 Is North America located closer to the North Pole or the South Pole?

3 Which continents does the Equator pass through?

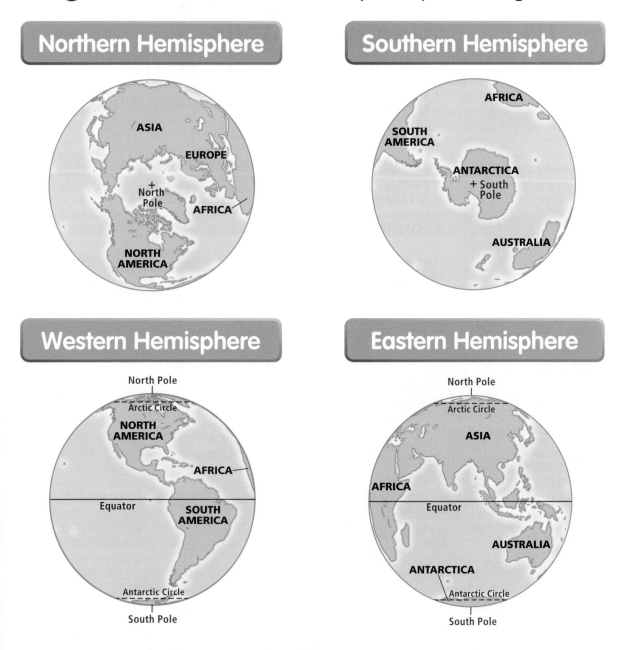

95

All Kinds of Communities

Vocabulary

city
urban area
suburb
rural area

Reading Skill

Main Idea and Details

STANDARDS
CORE: 2.3.03c Physical and human characteristics of neighborhood and community **2.6.02a** Families, groups, and communities influence lives and choices

Build on What You Know

Who are some people that live near you? These people are your neighbors.

Communities and Neighborhoods

Cities and towns are kinds of communities. A **city** is a place where many people live and work. A town is a community that is smaller than a city. A neighborhood is a smaller part of a community.

main idea

Many people live, work, and play in the city of Knoxville, Tennessee.

Most neighborhoods have homes. Some neighborhoods have stores, parks, and schools. People may work together to clean up their neighborhood. You can learn about being a good neighbor from the people around you.

(**Review**) What are two things most neighborhoods have?

Lee's map shows the places in his neighborhood. What kinds of buildings do people add to neighborhoods?

Urban Areas

Cars, trucks, and buses fill the streets in some cities. People build tall buildings, bridges, and railroads in urban areas. **Urban area** is another name for a city. Some urban areas also have natural features such as bodies of water and grassy parks.

main idea

The city of Nashville is on the Cumberland River.

Suburbs

Some people live in suburbs. A **suburb** is a community near a city. Cool Springs is a suburb of Nashville. People build homes, schools, and stores in suburbs.

main idea

The suburb of Cool Springs has many stores and businesses.

Suburbs can have ponds, lakes, and nature trails. People who live in suburbs may work in the city. Some people who live in Cool Springs work in Nashville. They can go to Nashville to have fun too.

Review What is one way that suburbs are the same as urban areas?

Rural Areas

Rural areas are outside of cities and suburbs. A **rural area** is a place that has more open space than a city or a suburb. People in rural areas may live in a small town. Small towns have fewer stores, schools, and homes than cities or suburbs. Greenville and Arlington are both rural towns in Tennessee.

Newport, Tennessee, is a rural area.

Farms

Most farms are in rural areas. Farmers need a lot of land to raise animals and to grow crops such as cotton and soybeans. Coopertown is a farming community in Middle Tennessee.

Review Why are farms in rural areas?

Tennessee has farms in all three of its Grand Divisions.

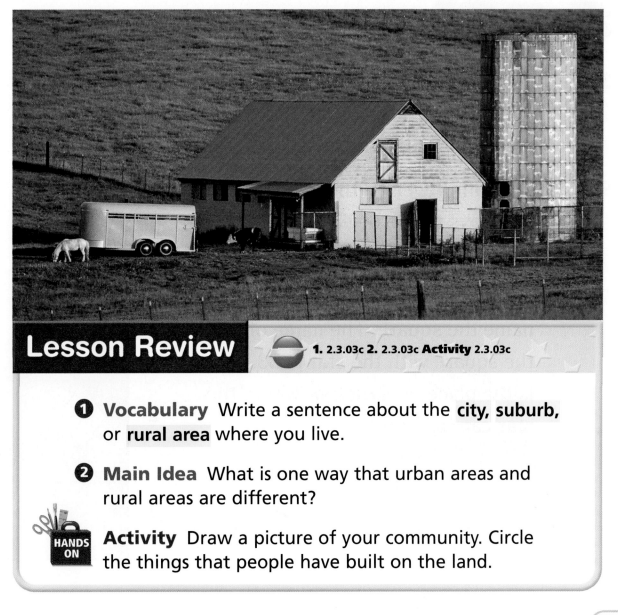

Lesson Review

1. 2.3.03c 2. 2.3.03c **Activity** 2.3.03c

❶ **Vocabulary** Write a sentence about the **city, suburb,** or **rural area** where you live.

❷ **Main Idea** What is one way that urban areas and rural areas are different?

HANDS ON

Activity Draw a picture of your community. Circle the things that people have built on the land.

Map and Globe Skills

Use a Grid

Grids can help you find places and things on maps. A **grid** is a pattern of lines. The lines make columns and rows. Each column has a letter, and each row has a number. The letters and the numbers name each square.

▶ **Vocabulary**

grid
location

Learn the Skill

Step 1 Look at this grid. Put your finger on the star. Move it straight up to the top of the column. What is the letter?

Step 2 Put your finger on the star again. Move it sideways to the beginning of the row. What is the number?

Step 3 Together, the letter and number name the square. The name of the square with the star is B3. That is the place, or **location,** where the star can be found.

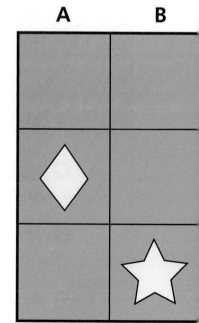

Practice the Skill

Look at the map. Then answer the questions.

1 Where is the library located? Name the square.

2 Where is the post office located? Name the square.

3 What is located in square D4?

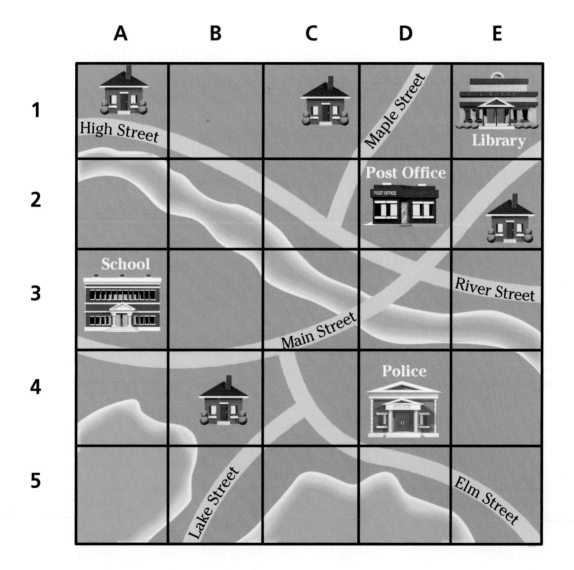

Land and Water

Build on What You Know

Think about your community. Is the land flat or hilly? Is there water nearby?

Landforms

main idea

Land on Earth has many different shapes. Each different shape is a **landform.** Hills and mountains are two kinds of landforms. The pictures on pages 104 to 105 show some different landforms.

Vocabulary
landform
valley
lake
river
barrier

Reading Skill
Compare and Contrast

STANDARDS
CORE: 2.3.02b Physical features define communities
EXTEND: 2.1.03a Poems, state cultural heritage

The Great Smoky Mountains in Tennessee

Great Smoky Mountains ▲

valley

mountain

valley

Appalachian Valley

mountains

The town of Gatlinburg, Tennessee, is in the Appalachian Valley.

A **valley** is low land between mountains or hills. A valley can be carved out of a mountain by a river running through it. More people choose to farm in valleys than on the steep sides of mountains.

Review Why do you think people would rather farm in valleys than on mountains?

Water

Water comes in many shapes and forms too. Most of Earth is covered with ocean water. Ocean water is salty. Most bodies of water on land are fresh water.

lake

A strong earthquake created Reelfoot Lake almost 200 years ago.

Reelfoot Lake

A **lake** is a body of water with land all around it. Most lakes have fresh water. Lakes come in many sizes. Some lakes are small. Others are very large. Reelfoot Lake is the largest natural lake in Tennessee.

river

Mississippi River

Skill What kind of land does the Mississippi River flow through in the photo above?

A **river** is a long, moving body of fresh water. Rivers flow downhill into oceans, lakes, or other rivers. The three biggest rivers in Tennessee are the Mississippi River, the Cumberland River, and the Tennessee River.

Review What is one way that lakes and rivers are different?

Barriers

Land and water can act as a barrier. A **barrier** (main idea ★) is something that separates two places. Landforms and water can be barriers between communities, states, or countries. The Mississippi River is a barrier between Tennessee and the states of Missouri and Arkansas. The Appalachian Mountains form a barrier between Tennessee and North Carolina.

Memphis

The Mississippi River acts as a barrier between Memphis, Tennessee and the state of Arkansas.

A riverbarge moves goods on the
Mississippi River.

Land and water affect how people live in a community.
The Mississippi River affects people in West Tennessee.
Farmers use the river to water their crops. People move
goods on the river from Tennessee to other states.

Review Why is the Mississippi River important to
Tennessee?

Lesson Review

1. 2.3.02b 2. 2.3.02b **Activity** 2.3.02b

❶ **Vocabulary** Write two sentences that tell what you
know about **landforms.**

❷ **Main Idea** List two ways that landforms and bodies
of water affect a community.

HANDS ON

Activity Draw a picture of one way people in your
community use land and water.

The Great Smokies

A legend is a story that is told and retold over many, many years. Joseph Bruchac retold this Cherokee legend about **landforms.**

If we should travel
far to the South,
there in the land
of mountains and mist,
we might hear the story
of how Earth was first shaped.

Water Beetle came out
to see if it was ready,
but the ground was
still as wet as a swamp,
too soft for anyone to stand.

Great Buzzard said, "I will help dry the land."
He began to fly close above the new Earth.
Where his wings came down,
valleys were formed,
and where his wings lifted,
hills rose up through the mist.

So the many rolling valleys and hills
of that place called the Great Smokies
came into being there.

Activities

1. **Talk About It** How does the Cherokee legend say that valleys were formed?

2. **Write About It** Make up a story about how another landform came to be.

111

Core Lesson 4

Regions

▶ **Vocabulary**

region
vegetation

⊙ **Reading Skill**

Main Idea and Details

STANDARDS

CORE: 2.3.01b Natural regions
maps: physical features, vegetation

Build on What You Know

What are some ways your community is different from or the same as a nearby community?

Regions

A **region** is an area that has some shared natural or human features. Some regions share natural features. Landform regions and plant regions are natural regions. Human regions share the features of the humans who live there. Two human regions are language regions and work regions.

main idea (★)

Mountains

Highlands

Landform Regions

Areas with shared landforms are landform regions. The United States has many landform regions. The map shows the main ones.

Review What is one landform region in Tennessee?

Skill **Reading Maps** Does the eastern or western part of the United States have more mountains?

Landform Regions of the United States

Map Key
- Plains
- Great Plains
- Highlands
- Mountains
- River
- Water

Plains

Water

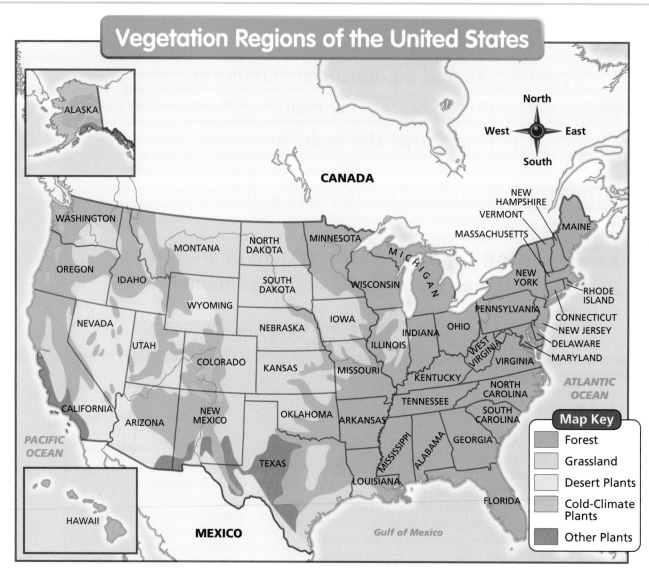

Vegetation Regions of the United States

Map Key
- Forest
- Grassland
- Desert Plants
- Cold-Climate Plants
- Other Plants

Which states have desert plants?

Vegetation Regions

Vegetation regions have the same kinds of plants. **Vegetation** means all the plants that grow naturally in an area. The United States has large forest regions and grassland regions. It also has regions with little vegetation. Some areas are too dry for most plants. Other regions are too cold and windy.

main ★ idea

Prickly pear cactus, a desert plant

Tennessee

Hawaii

The United States has many different forests. The forest in the picture on the left has the kinds of trees that grow in the forest region of Hawaii. The forest in the picture on the right has the kinds of trees that grow in Tennessee's mountain region.

Review What are two kinds of vegetation regions?

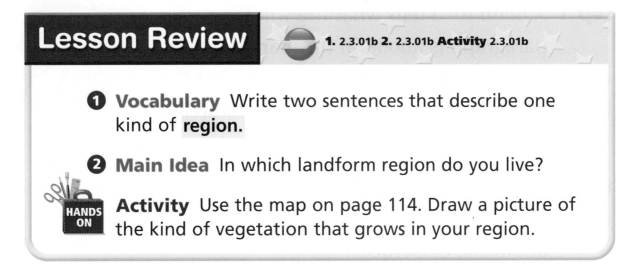

Lesson Review

1. 2.3.01b 2. 2.3.01b Activity 2.3.01b

❶ **Vocabulary** Write two sentences that describe one kind of **region.**

❷ **Main Idea** In which landform region do you live?

HANDS ON **Activity** Use the map on page 114. Draw a picture of the kind of vegetation that grows in your region.

Identify Main Idea and Details

▶ **Vocabulary**

main idea
detail

You just read about different regions. Knowing about main ideas and details can help you understand what you read.

Learn the Skill

Look for the **main idea** and **details** in this paragraph.

> Different kinds of trees grow in different regions of the United States. Honey mesquite (meh SKEET) trees grow where it is hot and dry. White spruce trees grow where it is cold in winter. Live oak trees grow in warm, wet regions.

Step 1 A **main idea** tells what the whole paragraph is about. In this paragraph, the first sentence tells the main idea. But the main idea can be any sentence that tells what the whole paragraph is about.

Step 2 The other sentences in this paragraph give the **details.** Each detail tells more about the main idea.

Live oak leaves and acorns

Read the paragraph below and look at the map.

1 Tell the main idea of this paragraph.

2 Give one detail from the paragraph and one detail from the map that tell more about the main idea.

Some regions of the United States get more rain than others. It rains the most on the northwest coast of the United States. The southeast region gets a lot of rain too. The southwest region gets the least rain.

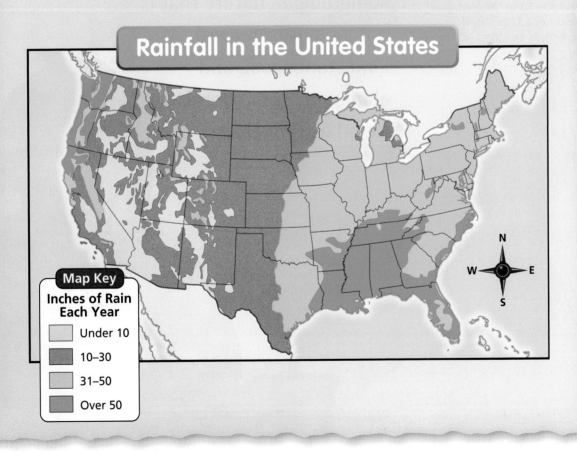

Rainfall in the United States

Map Key
Inches of Rain Each Year
Under 10
10–30
31–50
Over 50

N
W · E
S

People and the Environment

Vocabulary

mineral
environment

Reading Skill

Sequence

STANDARDS
CORE: 2.3.01b Natural regions maps:
natural resources **2.3.02a** People depend
on land resources **2.3.02e** Natural
resources: minerals, air, water, land

Build on What You Know

Most plants need air, soil, water, and sunlight. These are all found in nature.

Depending on Resources

People depend on natural resources. People use air, water, and land when they grow crops and raise animals. They use minerals for industry. A **mineral** is something in nature that is not a plant or animal. Limestone, coal, and aluminum are minerals found in Tennessee.

main
idea

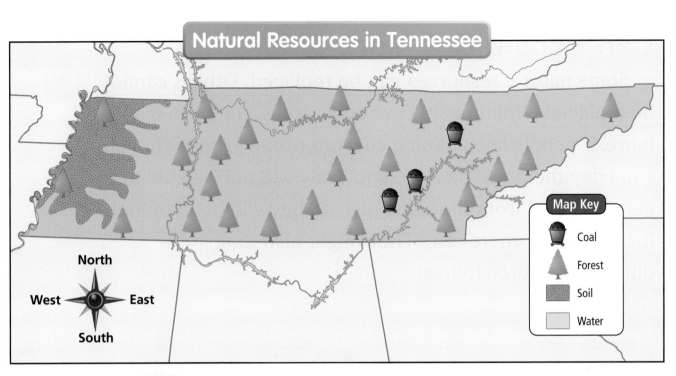

Natural Resources in Tennessee

North
West — East
South

Map Key

Coal

Forest

Soil

Water

Skill What are four natural resources found in Tennessee?

Tennessee's Natural Resources

Tennessee has many natural resources. Minerals, water, trees, and good soil are some of these resources. The land in Tennessee is very good for growing crops and raising animals. About half of the land in Tennessee has trees. People use wood from the trees to make paper and to build things.

main idea

Review In what ways do people in your community use natural resources?

Can People Get More of It?

Some natural resources can be replaced. Others cannot be replaced. When people cut down trees, they can plant more. If people keep mining coal out of the ground though, someday there will be none left. They will not be able to get more coal from the same place. They will need to look for coal somewhere else. They might also look for a different resource to use.

Resources that can be replaced

Trees

Resources that cannot be replaced

Coal

Changing the Environment

Land, water, people, and animals are part of the environment. The **environment** is the natural world around you. People can change their environment. They cut down trees to make room for new roads. They drain swamps and build new homes on the land.

Tennesseans built a dam across the Holston River to make Cherokee Reservoir.

Review What happens to the environment when people build homes or roads?

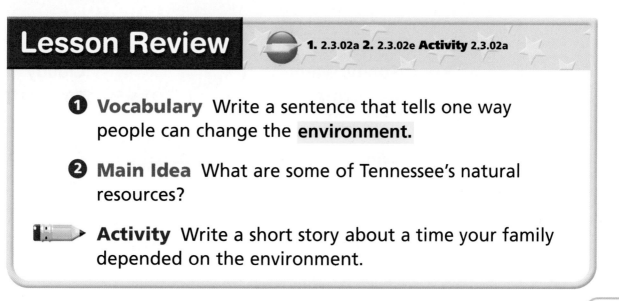

Lesson Review 1. 2.3.02a 2. 2.3.02e **Activity** 2.3.02a

❶ **Vocabulary** Write a sentence that tells one way people can change the **environment.**

❷ **Main Idea** What are some of Tennessee's natural resources?

Activity Write a short story about a time your family depended on the environment.

Weather and Climate

Vocabulary

weather
climate

Reading Skill

Main Idea and Details

STANDARDS
CORE: 2.3.01b Natural regions maps:
climate **2.3.02d** Hydrologic cycle

Build on What You Know

Is it raining, snowing, or sunny today? What it is like outside makes a difference in the activities you do each day.

Weather

Weather is what the air is like outside at any given time. People often want to know about weather because it affects their lives. Scientists measure weather in many ways. They also try to predict weather. Here is a weather report.

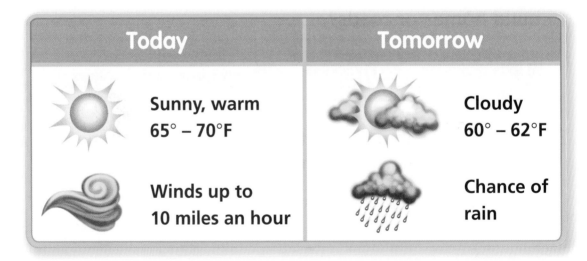

Today		Tomorrow	
☀	Sunny, warm 65° – 70°F	⛅	Cloudy 60° – 62°F
🌬	Winds up to 10 miles an hour	🌧	Chance of rain

Skill **Chart Reading** What do the words, numbers, and pictures tell about weather?

Climate

Climate is the usual weather of a place over a long time. A climate can have different kinds of weather. Jim and Jenna tell about the climate where they live.

July can be very hot in Milwaukee, Wisconsin.
Jim

January can be really cold.
Jim

Memphis, Tennessee has hot, humid summers.
Jenna

Rainstorms are part of our climate too.
Jenna

Review What are two kinds of weather that could be in one climate?

Living in Different Climates

Climates make a difference in the way people live. People in warm climates build homes that help them stay cool. The amount of rain and sun in a climate affects how people live too. Farmers need just the right amount of rain and sunlight to grow healthy crops. Rain does not just fall from the sky. Water moves in a circle from Earth to the sky and back to Earth again. This is called the water cycle.

main idea

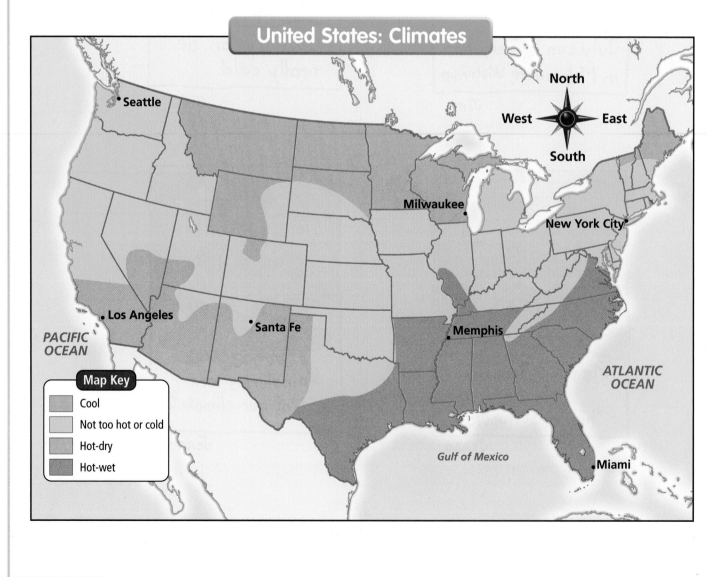

United States: Climates

North
West — East
South

Seattle

Milwaukee

New York City

Los Angeles

Santa Fe

Memphis

PACIFIC OCEAN

ATLANTIC OCEAN

Map Key
- Cool
- Not too hot or cold
- Hot-dry
- Hot-wet

Gulf of Mexico

Miami

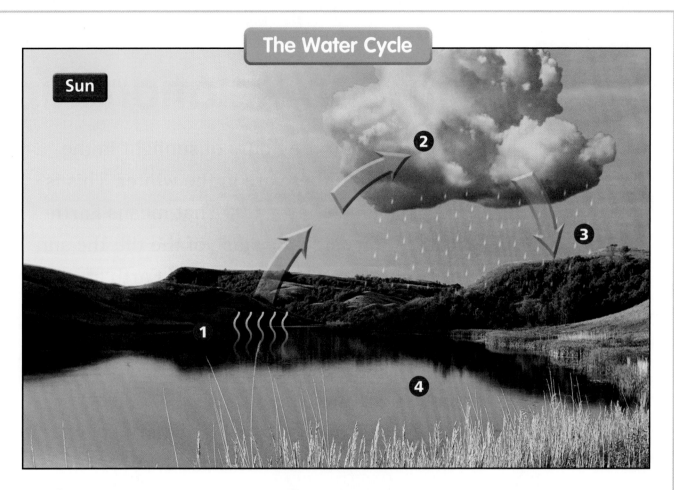

The Water Cycle

Sun

❶ The sun heats water. **❷** Water vapor forms clouds.
❸ Rain falls. **❹** Water collects in lake.

Review What is one way that climate
makes a difference in people's lives?

Lesson Review

1. 2.3.01b 2. 2.3.01b **Activity** 2.3.02d

❶ Vocabulary Write a sentence to explain the
difference between **weather** and **climate.**

❷ Main Idea In what way does climate make a
difference in how people live in your region?

Activity Make up a song to tell how the water
cycle works. Use a familiar tune for the song.

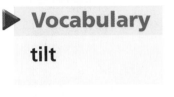

Skillbuilder

Earth-Sun Relationship

There are more hours of sunlight in the summer than there are in the winter. This is because Earth has a **tilt.** That means Earth leans to one side. Because of the tilt, the sun shines longer on some parts of Earth at different times of the year.

▶ **Vocabulary**

tilt

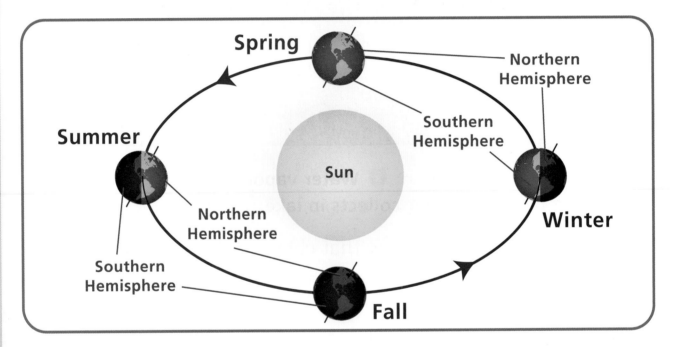

Spring

Northern Hemisphere

Southern Hemisphere

Sun

Summer

Northern Hemisphere

Southern Hemisphere

Fall

Winter

Learn the Skill

Step 1 Find the Northern Hemisphere in winter. Earth is tilted away from the sun during winter.

Step 2 Nashville, Tennessee is in the Northern Hemisphere. At what time of year is the Northern Hemisphere tilted toward the sun?

126 • Unit 3

Practice the Skill

Look at the chart. Then answer the questions.

1 About how many hours of light does Nashville get each day in the fall?

2 About how many hours of light does Nashville get each day in the spring?

Hours of Sunlight in Nashville

Season		Average Hours of Sunlight Each Day
Winter		11
Spring		13
Summer		13
Fall		11

Some Land and Water in North America

What are the missing words?

1. The large land shown on this map is the _____ of North America. **2.3.01c**

2. One large body of water on this map is the _____. **2.3.03a**

3. One landform shown on the map is _____. **2.3.01b**

4. You use a _____ _____ to know what the symbols on the map mean. **2.3.01d**

5. The map shows bodies of water such as oceans, lakes, and _____. **2.3.03a**

Vocabulary

Choose the missing word in each sentence.

6. A _____ is low land between hills or mountains. 2.3.01b

7. A city may also be called a(n) _____. 2.3.03c

8. The _____ is the natural world around us. 2.3.02e

9. _____ is the usual weather of a place over a long period of time. 2.3.03c

A. **climate** (page 123)

B. **region** (page 112)

C. **valley** (page 105)

D. **urban area** (page 98)

E. **environment** (page 121)

Critical Thinking

10. Describe a way that people have changed the environment. 2.3.02a

11. Describe a way that people depend on the environment. 2.3.02a

12. What are some ways that a suburb is the same as a rural area? 2.3.03c

Unit Project

★ The Big Idea

Keep a Weather Log

Keep track of the weather for a week. Use that information to make a weather log.

❶ Draw a picture to show the kind of weather each day.

❷ Note whether it is cloudy, sunny, raining, or snowing.

2.3.02c

CURRENT EVENTS
WEEKLY (WR) READER

Current Events Project

Find information about places in regions throughout the United States. Make a **3-D Landform Map** for each region.

The Sierra Nevada Mountains

2.3.02b

Technology

Read articles about current events at www.eduplace.com/kids/hmss/

Parts of a Globe

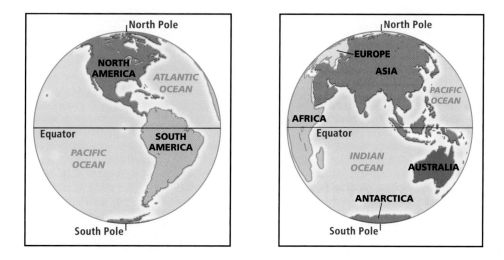

Directions

Use the globes above and what you know to do Numbers 13 and 14.

13 Which two continents are completely in the Southern Hemisphere? **2.3.01a**

(A) North America and South America

(B) Australia and Antarctica

(C) South America and Africa

(D) Europe and Asia

14 Which two continents does the Equator pass through? **2.3.01a**

(A) North America and Antarctica

(B) South America and Australia

(C) Europe and Asia

(D) South America and Africa

Government

> **"My country 'tis of thee,
> Sweet land of liberty,
> Of thee I sing."**
>
> —Samuel Francis Smith
> from "America"

The Big Idea

What does government mean to you and your family?

Unit 4 Government

Vocabulary Preview

Technology
e • glossary
e • word games
www.eduplace.com/kids/hmss/

government

Government is a group of people who run a community, state, or country.

page 136

citizen

A **citizen** is a member of a community, state, or country. You are also a citizen of your class. page 142

Reading Strategy

Use the **summarize** reading strategy in Lessons 1, 2, and 3 and the **question** strategy in Lessons 4 and 5.

authority

Authority is a right to do something. Police officers have the authority to make sure people follow the law.

page 154

monument

A **monument** is something, such as a building or statue, that honors a hero or event.

page 168

135

Government and People

STANDARDS
CORE: 2.4.01b Functions of governments **2.4.01c** Every community has a form of goverance **2.4.04a** Government services in the community **2.4.04b** Citizens fund community services

Vocabulary

government
capital
taxes

Reading Skill

Main Idea and Details

Build on What You Know

Who are the people who run your school? What are some ways they work together?

What Is Government?

A **government** is a group of people who work together to run a community, state, or country. A government works to keep order, keep people safe, and solve problems.

CITY OF CHATTANOOGA

These people run the city of Chattanooga, Tennessee.

The leaders of local government in Farragut, Tennessee, work at this town hall.

Local Government

Every community has some kind of government. The government of a community is called a local government. A local government is made up of people from the community. They decide how to use money for schools, safety, and other community needs. They try to solve community problems too.

main (★) idea

Review What do people in a local government do?

Three Governments

Your state also has a government. Each state has a **capital,** which is a city where the people in government work. The United States has a government too. That is the national government. It is in Washington, D.C., the nation's capital. Everyone has three governments: local, state, and national.

main idea

I live in Farragut, Tennessee. Leaders of my **local** government meet in Farragut.

Leaders of my **state** government meet in Nashville, the capital of Tennessee.

Leaders of my **national** government meet in Washington, D.C.

The United States of America

CANADA

North
West — East
South

NORTH DAKOTA
★Bismarck

MINNESOTA
St. Paul★

SOUTH DAKOTA
★Pierre

WISCONSIN
Madison★

MICHIGAN
★Lansing

NEW HAMPSHIRE
VERMONT
Montpelier★
Concord★

MAINE
Augusta★

MASSACHUSETTS
★Boston
★Providence

NEW YORK
Albany★
Hartford★
RHODE ISLAND
CONNECTICUT

Cheyenne★

NEBRASKA
Lincoln★

IOWA
Des Moines★

ILLINOIS
Springfield★

INDIANA
Indianapolis★

OHIO
Columbus★

PENNSYLVANIA
Harrisburg★
★Trenton
NEW JERSEY

Denver★

COLORADO

Topeka★

KANSAS

MISSOURI
Jefferson City★

Annapolis★
Dover★
⊛Washington, D.C.
DELAWARE
MARYLAND

WEST VIRGINIA
Charleston★

Richmond★
VIRGINIA

KENTUCKY
Frankfort★

•Farragut
Raleigh★
NORTH CAROLINA

ATLANTIC OCEAN

OKLAHOMA
Oklahoma City★

ARKANSAS
Little Rock★

TENNESSEE
Nashville★

Columbia★
SOUTH CAROLINA

Atlanta★

TEXAS

MISSISSIPPI
Jackson★

ALABAMA
Montgomery★

GEORGIA

LOUISIANA
Baton Rouge★

★Tallahassee

Austin★

FLORIDA

MEXICO

Gulf of Mexico

Map Key
• City
★ State capital
⊛ National capital
— State boundary
— National boundary

Skill **Reading Maps** Find Farragut, Tennessee. Is Farragut east or west of Tennessee's state capital?

Review What three governments do you have?

Government Services

Think about the services you read about in Unit 2. Fixing cars and cutting hair are services. Governments have many services for people too. Local, state, and national governments each help with different services.

main idea (★)

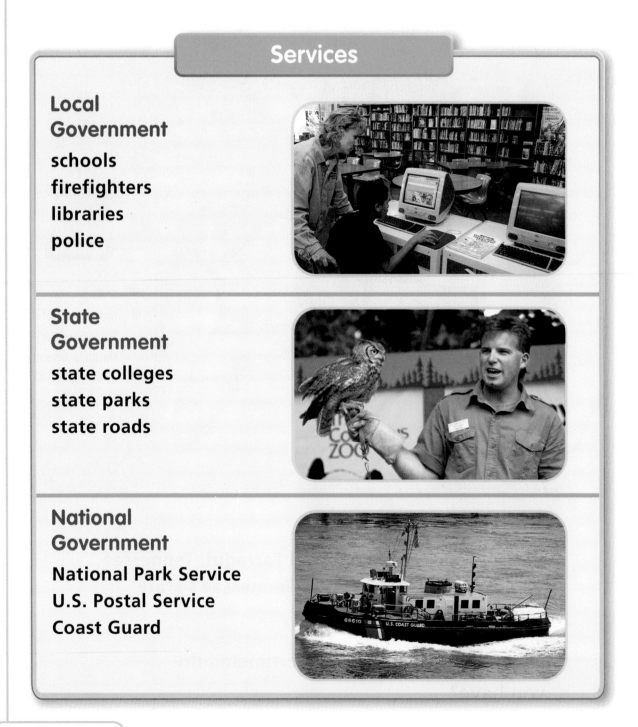

Services

Local Government

schools
firefighters
libraries
police

State Government

state colleges
state parks
state roads

National Government

National Park Service
U.S. Postal Service
Coast Guard

Taxes

To pay for services, governments collect money called taxes. **Taxes** are money people pay to the government. Governments use money from taxes to pay for services such as parks, police, and roads. Workers pay income taxes from the money they earn. Businesses also pay income taxes. In most states, people pay sales taxes when they buy goods.

main idea

Review Why do governments need money from taxes?

Baseball Bat	35.00
Baseball	8.00
Baseball glove	40.00
SUBTOTAL	83.00
Tennessee Tax 7.00%	5.81
TOTAL	$88.81
Cash	90.00
Cash Change	1.19

Lesson Review

1. 2.4.04b 2. 2.4.01c, 2.4.02d **Activity** 2.4.04a

❶ **Vocabulary** Write a sentence that explains what **taxes** are.

❷ **Main Idea** What are the three governments that people have?

▶ **Activity** Write or tell about a local government service you use. Explain how it helps you and other people.

Citizens Make a Difference

Vocabulary
citizen
right
volunteer
justice

Reading Skill
Classify

STANDARDS
CORE: 2.4.03a Good citizenship; justice, truth, equality, and responsibility **2.4.03b** Qualities of good citizenship **2.4.03c** Identify good citizens
EXTEND: 2.4.01a Groups work for order and security **2.6.01a** Work independently and cooperatively

Build on What You Know

How have students and adults made your school a good place to learn?

You Are a Citizen

You are a citizen of the community where you live and the nation where you were born. A **citizen** is a person who belongs to a place. Citizens have rights. A **right** is something that you are allowed to do by law.

main ★ idea

RIGHTS

Speak Freely   Worship   Be Equal

Betsy and Dan are volunteers. They collect turkeys and give them to families who have no money to buy Thanksgiving dinner.

Some people volunteer in groups. They work to make the community better for everyone.

Being a Good Citizen

Good citizens work together to help their communities. They care about others. They try to make things fair and safe for everyone. There are many ways to be a good citizen. You can follow rules or do chores. You can also be a volunteer. A **volunteer** does a job without being paid. Volunteers can work alone or with a group of people to get things done.

main ★ idea

Review How can you be a good citizen?

Everyday Good Citizens

People show good citizenship in communities every day. Good citizenship is being respectful in your home, school, and community. People in Tennessee do different things to show good citizenship.

main idea

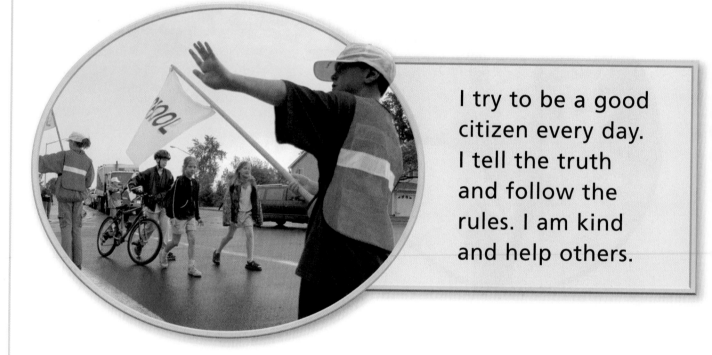

I try to be a good citizen every day. I tell the truth and follow the rules. I am kind and help others.

I am a teacher. I make sure all students in my class have the same rights, or equality.

JUDGE D'ARMY BAILEY

I am a judge. To be a good citizen, I must treat everyone with justice. **Justice** means fairness.

Review In what ways does a judge show good citizenship?

Lesson Review 1. 2.4.03a 2. 2.4.03b **Activity** 2.4.03c

❶ **Vocabulary** Use the word **justice** in a sentence about being a good citizen.

❷ **Main Idea** Why is it important to show good citizenship?

HANDS ON **Activity** Make a poster that shows someone being a good citizen. Write sentences to explain how this person is helping the school, community, or nation.

145

A Pesky Problem

Read about some citizens who show responsibility by working together to solve a problem in their neighborhood.

Cast	
Narrator	**Mary**
Pablo	**Mr. Kwan**
Latoya	**Mrs. Kwan**

Scene 1

Narrator: Good citizens work together to solve problems and to keep people safe. The citizens of Oak Street come together to solve their problem.

Mr. Kwan: Those raccoons did it again! They knocked over our trash can.

Pablo: Sounds like you have a big problem, Mr. Kwan.

Latoya: Those raccoons are making a mess all over the neighborhood! They got into our trash can too. We'll help you clean up.

Mrs. Kwan: Thank you. I wish you could help us solve this pesky problem.

Mary: Maybe we can if we work together.

Mrs. Kwan: But what can we do?

Latoya: I have an idea. Let's ask the town council to help.

Mr. Kwan: It might work. We can let the town council know that these raccoons bother everyone on Oak Street.

Scene 2

Narrator: The neighborhood group met with the town council. The council told them to buy trash cans with special tight-fitting lids.

Mary: The town council had a good idea, but those special trash cans are expensive!

Mrs. Kwan: Maybe the town could buy the trash cans.

Latoya: Or each family could hold a yard sale to raise money for their own trash can.

Pablo: Maybe we could have a neighborhood bake sale.

Mr. Kwan: What great ideas!

How to Solve a Problem
1. Name the problem.

2. List ways to solve it.

3. Choose the best way.

4. Find out if it solves the problem.

Mrs. Kwan: Let's have a neighborhood meeting. We can decide if each family is going to solve this problem alone or if the families of Oak Street will work together as a group.

Pablo: I'll make flyers so that everyone knows about the meeting.

Latoya: I have a feeling this pesky problem is about to be solved!

Activities

1. **Talk About It** What ways did the citizens work together to solve their problem?

2. **Write About It** Think about what might happen next. Write another scene for the play.

Identify Cause and Effect

▶ **Vocabulary**

cause
effect

Citizens can work together to solve problems. Why might one group of citizens work together to clean and fix things at a park? Knowing about cause and effect can help you understand why things happen.

Learn the Skill

A **cause** makes something happen. Something that happens is an **effect**.

cause ➡ effect

Step 1 Look at the *Cause* picture. There is trash on the ground. Litter is one cause for the citizens to work together to clean the park.

Step 2 Look at the *Effect* picture. The effect of the citizens cleaning the park is that it is clean and safe.

Step 3 You can explain cause and effect using the word **because.** Citizens cleaned up the park **because** it had trash on the ground.

Practice the Skill

Follow the directions to identify cause and effect.

1 Look at the *Effect* picture. What did the citizens do to the park that caused it to look so different?

2 Think about what you learned. Look at the pictures. What are two causes for why people worked together to clean and fix things at this park?

Cause

Effect

Laws

Build on What You Know

What are some rules in your school or classroom? Communities, states, and countries have rules too.

Laws Are Important

Governments make laws. A **law** is a rule that everyone in a community, state, or country must follow. Laws keep order. They also keep people safe. They help people get along with one another.

main idea

STANDARDS
CORE: 2.4.01d Governments establish order, provide security, and manage conflict **2.4.02a** Communities have different laws **2.4.02b** People make and enforce laws in Tennessee
EXTEND: 2.4.03c Ordinary people, good citizenship

Vocabulary
law
duty
authority

Reading Skill
Main Idea and Details

The signs on this page tell people about laws.

DO NOT FEED THE ANIMALS

SCHOOL ZONE

STOP

Most states have laws about wearing seatbelts.

Traffic laws help keep people safe.

Community Laws

Every community has its own set of laws. Each local government makes laws to solve problems for its community. Citizens have a duty to follow the laws of their community. A **duty** is something a person should do. Citizens also have a duty to follow the laws of their state and nation.

(main ★ idea)

Review Why are laws important?

These people work together to make laws for Tennessee.

Who Makes Laws?

Government leaders help make community, state, and national laws. Only certain leaders have the authority to make laws. **Authority** is a right to do something. Local government leaders make laws for each community. Leaders in the state government make state laws. People from Tennessee and other states work together to make national laws.

Following Laws

Judges and police help with laws. Police tell people how to follow the law. They stop people who break laws. A judge helps if a person has broken a law. A judge decides what a person must do to make up for breaking a law.

Review In what ways do police and judges help with laws?

Judges work in courts. Here two lawyers talk to a judge.

Police stop drivers who speed.

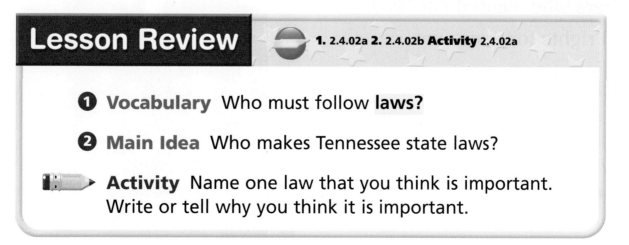

Lesson Review

1. 2.4.02a 2. 2.4.02b **Activity** 2.4.02a

❶ **Vocabulary** Who must follow **laws?**

❷ **Main Idea** Who makes Tennessee state laws?

▶ **Activity** Name one law that you think is important. Write or tell why you think it is important.

Rosa Parks

Rosa Parks in 1999

Not everyone is brave enough to risk going to jail for what they believe is right. In 1955, Rosa Parks showed courage when she stood up for her beliefs.

At that time Rosa Parks was living in Montgomery, Alabama. The state's **laws** and rules did not give black people the same rights as white people. This seemed very wrong to Rosa Parks. She began to work with others who wanted fair laws and rights for everyone.

Rosa Parks helped change a law that was unfair to African American people on buses.

Taking Action

On December 1, 1955, Rosa Parks acted against an unfair law. The law made black people give up their bus seats to white people.

Rosa Parks stayed firmly in her seat when the bus driver tried to make her give it up. She had to go to jail for this. Her action led many others to work together to change the unfair law.

Activities

1. **Talk About It** How did Rosa Parks show courage?

2. **Build It** Make a mobile that shows pictures of citizens who did something brave.

Leaders

Build on What You Know

Government leaders make laws. What are some other jobs that leaders in your school and community do?

Vocabulary

vote
election
qualification
privilege

Reading Skill

Sequence

Choosing Leaders

Did you ever choose a leader for a team? When you show or write a choice, you **vote.** Your school might have an **election.** That is a time when people vote. When you turn eighteen, you will have the right to vote in government elections. All three kinds of government have elections.

STANDARDS
CORE: 2.4.02c Ways public officials are selected; election, appointment **2.4.02d** Local, state, and national governments; leaders; mayor, governor, and president

Vote for Tina for Class President

Government Leaders

Local Government

Citizens may vote for **mayor** of their city or town.

State Government

Citizens may vote for **governor** of the state where they live.

National Government

Citizens may vote for **President** of the United States.

Government leaders have important jobs. In elections, citizens get to choose leaders who they think can do these jobs the best. Sometimes leaders appoint people to government jobs. To appoint means that a person is chosen for a job without an election.

main (★) idea

Review Why do citizens vote?

Before You Vote

Citizens should choose a leader with the best qualifications. A **qualification** is a skill that makes a person good for a job. Citizens learn about a leader's qualifications by reading newspapers, watching television, and asking questions.

Will you add more bus stops?

What can you do to fix our playgrounds?

My Questions

★ Is this person honest and smart?

★ Will this person work hard for all citizens?

★ Can this person run the government best?

A Right and Responsibility

Voting is a privilege. A **privilege** is another word for right. Voting is also a duty. <u>Citizens have the right and duty, or responsibility, to vote for their local, state, and national leaders.</u>

Review Why should citizens learn about a leader's qualifications?

Good citizens vote for the leaders they think will do the best job.

Lesson Review

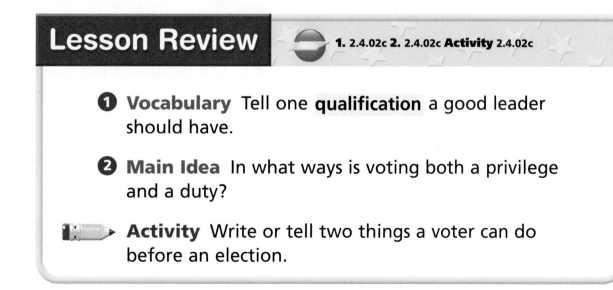

1. 2.4.02c 2. 2.4.02c **Activity** 2.4.02c

❶ Vocabulary Tell one **qualification** a good leader should have.

❷ Main Idea In what ways is voting both a privilege and a duty?

Activity Write or tell two things a voter can do before an election.

Citizenship Skills

Skillbuilder

Make a Decision

Good citizens and leaders think before they make decisions. They listen to other people's ideas. When you make a **decision,** you make up your mind. Comparing choices in a chart can help you make a good decision.

▶ **Vocabulary**

decision

Learn the Skill

Suppose that your class has two different ideas about projects to help the school. How do you make a decision about which projects to do?

Step 1 Make a chart that shows the two ideas.

Step 2 Think about what is good and not good about each choice. Use plus (+) for good and minus (-) for not good. Write your thoughts in the chart.

Step 3 Compare choices in the chart. You might ask: Which choice will help more people in the school? Decide which choice is better.

School Clean-up Day	School Garden
+ School will look better. More school pride	**+** Beautiful flowers Healthful vegetables
− Hard work Not fun	**−** Takes too long. Might not grow.

Practice the Skill

Follow the directions. Then make a decision about who you might vote for.

1 Look at the pictures and read the words. Tell what the choices are for class leader.

2 Make a chart to show what is good about each choice and what is not good about each choice.

3 Think of a question you might ask to help you decide. Use the question and the chart to make a choice.

Vote for Marie.
She wants a
new soccer field.

Vote for Peter.
He is a leader
who listens to
everyone.

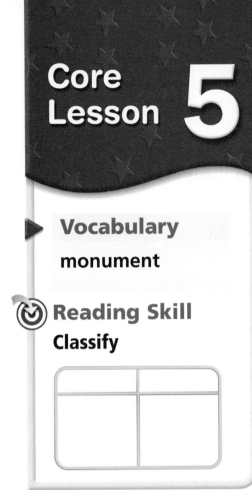

STANDARDS

CORE: 2.1.03a State cultural heritage **2.4.04c** Patriotic symbols and landmarks of Tennessee **2.5.03a** Community landmarks

What are some symbols on the seal of the President of the United States?

Symbols

Build on What You Know

What would you put in a picture to stand for the United States or Tennessee? Pictures, buildings, and statues are symbols that can stand for a country or state.

United States Symbols

Our country has many symbols. A symbol is a picture, place, or thing that stands for something else. For example, the bald eagle on a quarter stands for a strong country.

Symbols for the United States remind people that they are part of one country. The American flag is the symbol people use most often for the United States. The flag has red and white stripes. It has 50 stars, one for each state.

main idea

Review Why are symbols for the United States important to people who live here?

Uncle Sam is a symbol for the United States.

Tennessee Symbols

The state of Tennessee has its own symbols. The symbols show things that are important to the people of Tennessee.

The Tennessee state seal shows that farming and trade are important in the state.

farming

trade

The iris is the state flower of Tennessee.

The Tennessee state quarter shows musical instruments. What are their names?

The three stars on the Tennessee state flag
are symbols of the three grand divisions.
Each division has different land and culture.

The raccoon is the state
animal of Tennessee.

Monuments and Landmarks

Places can be symbols too. Many buildings and statues help us remember people and events from Tennessee's past. Some of these symbols are monuments. A **monument** can be a building, statue, or landmark that honors people or events.

(★) main idea

James White's Fort

Knoxville, Tennessee

Over two hundred years ago, James White built the first house in the area that is now Knoxville. People can visit his log house. The house reminds people of early Tennessee settlers.

W.C. Handy Statue

Memphis, Tennessee

W.C. Handy was known as the "Father of the Blues." He became famous for his music in Memphis. He wrote a song called the *Memphis Blues*. The city of Memphis built this statue as a monument to honor him.

Tennessee State Capitol

Nashville, Tennessee

This is the Tennessee State Capitol. It was built in Nashville over 100 years ago. It is one of the oldest capitols in the United States that is still used. This landmark is where Tennessee leaders work and make laws.

Review What is important about the Tennessee State Capitol?

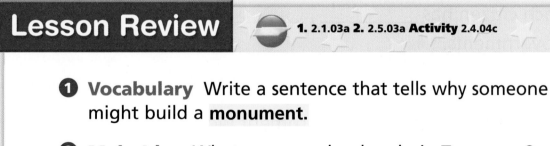

Lesson Review

1. 2.1.03a 2. 2.5.03a **Activity** 2.4.04c

❶ **Vocabulary** Write a sentence that tells why someone might build a **monument.**

❷ **Main Idea** What are some landmarks in Tennessee?

Activity Draw a new symbol for Tennessee. Tell what you think and feel about the symbol.

Big Idea   The Big Idea

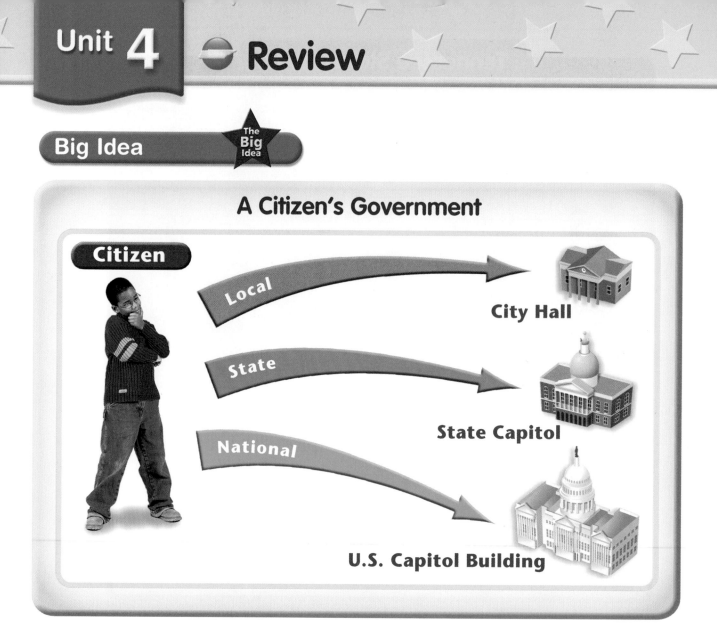

A Citizen's Government

Citizen

Local → City Hall

State → State Capitol

National → U.S. Capitol Building

Fill in the missing words that help describe the chart.

1. Every community has some kind of _____. 2.4.01c

2. Each citizen has _____ , _____ , and _____ governments. 2.4.02d

3. Leaders in state government work at the _____. 2.4.02d

4. Leaders in the national government work in the _____. 2.4.02d

5. Citizens _____ in an election to choose their leaders. 2.4.02c

Vocabulary

Write the letter of the correct answer.

6. The money that people pay to a government 2.4.04b

7. A person who belongs to a place 2.4.03b

8. A freedom that government must protect 2.4.01d

9. A time when people vote 2.4.02c

A. **right** (page 142)

B. **election** (page 158)

C. **taxes** (page 141)

D. **citizen** (page 142)

E. **justice** (page 145)

Critical Thinking

10. In what way is your local government like your national government? 2.4.01b, 2.4.01d, 2.4.02d

11. In what way is your local government different from your national government? 2.4.01b, 2.4.01d, 2.4.02d

12. Explain the difference between a duty and a privilege. 2.4.03b

Review

Unit Project

The Big Idea

Make Up a Riddle

Think of a person, place, or thing you learned about in this unit. You might choose a government leader or monument. Keep your choice secret.

1 Fold a sheet of paper in half and write two riddle clues on the outside. Write your secret answer inside.

2 Show your clues to others. Can they guess?

2.4.02d

CURRENT EVENTS
WEEKLY (WR) READER

Current Events Project

Find out what your local government is doing. Make a **Government in the News Big Book.**

2.4.01c

Technology

Read articles about current events at www.eduplace.com/kids/hmss/

Directions

Mrs. Tan's class chose a place for a field trip. Use their pictograph and what you know to do Numbers 13 and 14.

Votes for Our Field Trip

Aquarium	✔✔✔✔✔✔✔
Fire Station	✔✔✔
Bakery	✔✔✔✔
Dairy Farm	✔✔✔✔✔✔

13 Which choice has the most votes?   2.4.02c

(A) Aquarium

(B) Fire Station

(C) Bakery

(D) Dairy Farm

14 Which of these is an example of how to find out the number of votes?   2.4.02c

(A) Read the top rows.

(B) Read the left column.

(C) Count the Bakery check marks.

(D) Count all the check marks.

UNIT 5

In the Past

"The world is full of stories, and from time to time they permit themselves to be told"

—Old Cherokee saying

The Big Idea

Why is the past important to you today?

Unit 5 In the Past

Vocabulary Preview

Technology

e • **glossary**
e • **word games**
www.eduplace.com/kids/hmss/

technology

Technology is the use of science to make new things or to make things work better. page 191

history

History is everything we can know about the past. The invention of writing was an important event in history. page 180

Reading Strategy

Use the **predict and infer** reading strategy in Lessons 1, 2, and 3 and the **monitor and clarify** strategy in Lessons 4 and 5.

artifact

An **artifact** is a thing that was made by people in the past. Artifacts help us learn what was important to people long ago. **page 192**

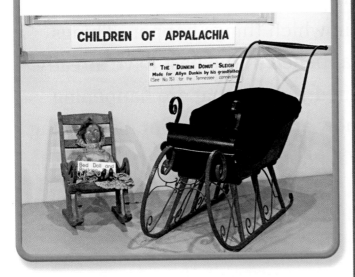

hero

A **hero** is someone who does something brave for the good of others. Alvin York is a hero from Tennessee. **page 202**

Looking at Time

Vocabulary

chronology
ancient times
modern times
history

Reading Skill

Sequence

STANDARDS
CORE: 2.5.02a Ancient times and modern times
2.5.02b Chronology: past, present and future
EXTEND: 2.5.02b Chronology: past, present and future
2.5.02d Communities change over time

Build on What You Know

How old are you? Your age now is in the present. You will be a grownup in the future. You were a baby in the past.

Talking About Time

People use many words to talk about time and chronology. **Chronology** is the order in which things happen. Things that happened in the **past** have already happened. Things that are happening right now are in the **present.** Something that will happen later is in the **future.**

Marisa,
age 6 months

Marisa, age 8

Marisa, age 25

Ancient and Modern Times

People use different words to talk about time. Ancient times were a long, long time ago in the past. People in ancient times did not have the tools that we have today. We live in modern times. **Modern times** are now and just a few years in the past. We have many tools that make our lives easier.

In ancient times, people wrote letters using a pointed stick to mark on a clay slab.

In modern times, people can use computers to type letters quickly.

History

You can learn about ancient times and modern times by studying history. **History** is what we can know about the past. It is everything that has happened in places and in the lives of people from far back in the past up to the present.

A storyteller in Alaska uses his drum to tell young people stories from the past.

Everyone and every place has a history. You have a history. Your family has a history. Communities, states, and countries have histories too.

Review What are some things that have happened in your own history?

Lesson Review

1. 2.5.02b 2. 2.5.02a **Activity** 2.5.02b

❶ **Vocabulary** Write a sentence using the word **chronology.**

❷ **Main Idea** What is one way that modern times are different from ancient times?

Activity Make a three-part picture of your life. Show something that you did in the past, present, and what you hope you will do in the future.

A City Grows Taller

Three hundred years ago, Knoxville was not the city it is today. It was not even a town. At first Cherokee Indians hunted on the land. Then settlers came. They built homes and farms.

Knoxville today

Over time, more people moved to Knoxville. They built homes, schools, and other buildings. Knoxville became a city. The city started to run out of open space. The people of Knoxville built skyscrapers. The skyscrapers used little land and space. They held many more people and businesses. They still do today.

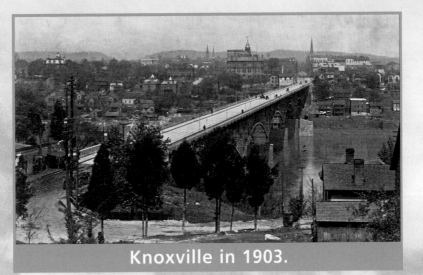

Knoxville in 1903.

Activities

1. **Talk About It** Why did Knoxville grow taller?

2. **Draw It** Draw a picture of what your community might look like 50 years in the future.

Skillbuilder

Read a Timeline

▶ **Vocabulary**

timeline

A timeline can show the chronology of a family's history. A **timeline** is an ordered group of words and dates that shows when events happened. Look at the timeline of Andrea's family.

Learn the Skill

Step 1 The title tells what the timeline is about. The timeline has a line divided in equal parts. Each part stands for 10 years.

Step 2 Look at the first and last numbers on the timeline. The numbers are years. The events on the timeline happened between these years.

Step 3 The numbers with the events on the timeline tell the year in which each event happened.

1930   1940   1950

1946
Andrea's grand-father is born.

1935
Andrea's great-grandmother comes to the United States from Japan.

Practice the Skill

Use the timeline to answer the questions below.

1 Was Andrea's grandfather born before or after her great-grandmother came to the United States?

2 When did Andrea's great-grandmother come to the United States?

3 What happened in 1994?

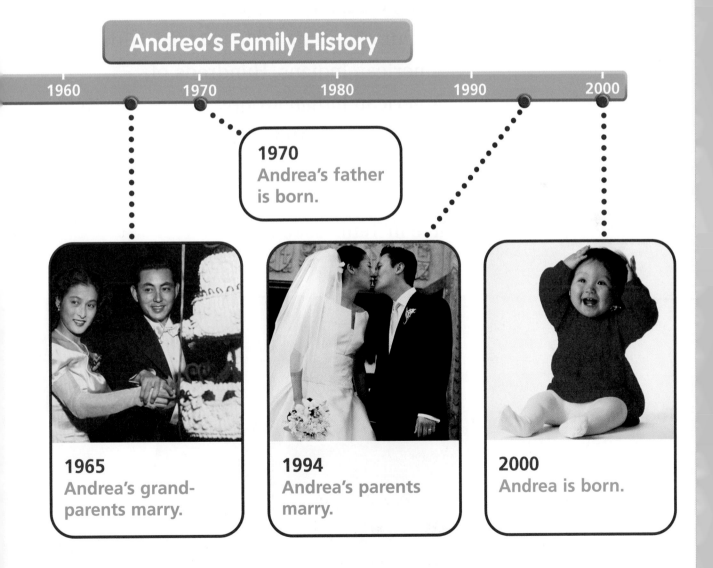

Andrea's Family History

1960   1970   1980   1990   2000

1970
Andrea's father is born.

1965
Andrea's grand-parents marry.

1994
Andrea's parents marry.

2000
Andrea is born.

185

► **Vocabulary**

settlement
transportation
technology

Reading Skill
Classify

STANDARDS
CORE: 2.1.03b Changing
technologies on local community
and state **2.5.02d** Communities
change over time

Today, Choctaw
share their culture
by passing on
their language.

Communities Change

Build on What You Know

In what ways do you think life in your community was different in the past than it is in the present?

First Americans

Our country's history starts with American Indians. Hundreds of American Indian groups lived in North America more than 500 years ago. The Cherokee, Choctaw, and Chickasaw are three American Indian groups that still live in Tennessee today.

Settlements

People came from Europe to North America more than 500 years ago. They formed settlements near American Indians already living on the land. A **settlement** is a small community. Plymouth and Jamestown were two settlements. People built homes, farms, and churches. Over time, people decided to form a new country called the United States of America.

Review What did the Europeans build in North American settlements?

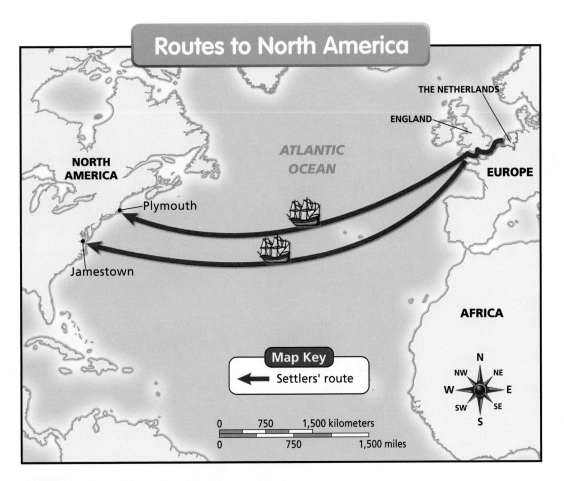

Routes to North America

THE NETHERLANDS

ENGLAND

ATLANTIC OCEAN

NORTH AMERICA

EUROPE

Plymouth

Jamestown

AFRICA

Map Key

Settlers' route

N
NW   NE
W   E
SW   SE
S

0   750   1,500 kilometers
0   750   1,500 miles

Skill **Reading Maps** From which countries in Europe did first settlers come?

Communities Change

The United States became a nation more than 200 years ago. At first, there were few cities or roads. There were no tall buildings. Over many years, people built communities across the country. They built bridges, roads, businesses, and schools. People in the United States have changed their communities over the past 200 years.

This warehouse was built to hold tools for workers who were building a bridge across the Clinch River in Tennessee.

You can see how a community has changed by comparing maps. These two maps show changes in the community of Plainfield, Illinois. Compare the roads on both maps.

Illinois

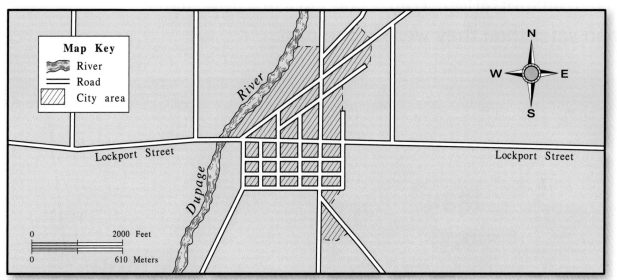

Map Key
- River
- Road
- City area

Lockport Street

Lockport Street

River

Dupage

N
W E
S

0   2000 Feet
0   610 Meters

Plainfield, Illinois, more than 100 years ago

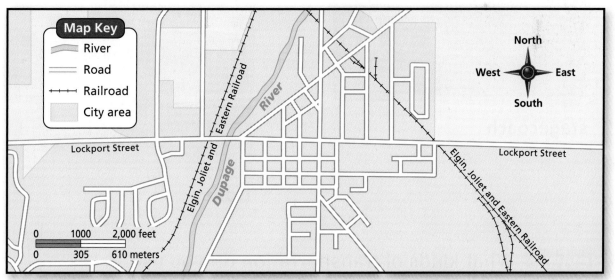

Map Key
- River
- Road
- Railroad
- City area

Lockport Street

Lockport Street

River

Dupage

Elgin, Joliet and Eastern Railroad

Elgin, Joliet and Eastern Railroad

North
West East
South

0   1000   2,000 feet
0   305   610 meters

Plainfield today

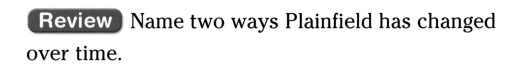

Review Name two ways Plainfield has changed over time.

Technology Changes Communities

Transportation has changed a lot since the United States became a country. **Transportation** is any way of moving things or people from one place to another. When people travel or move goods, they use transportation. Trains and cars are now faster and safer than they were in the past.

1850   1900

1834

stagecoach

1904

trolley

Review What kinds of transportation do you use?

People use technology to make new kinds of transportation. **Technology** is using science to make things work better. New kinds of technology and transportation change how people live in a community.

main idea (★)

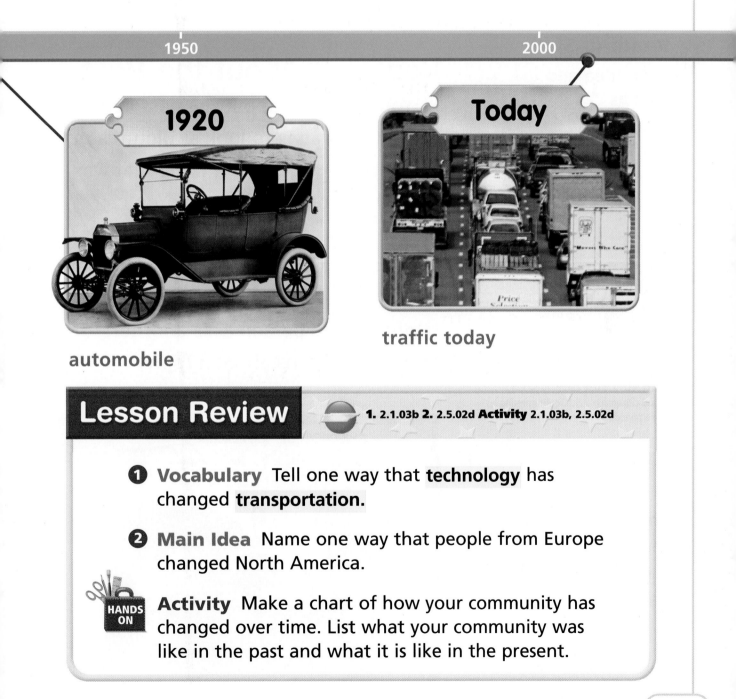

1950

2000

1920

automobile

Today

traffic today

Lesson Review

1. 2.1.03b 2. 2.5.02d **Activity** 2.1.03b, 2.5.02d

❶ **Vocabulary** Tell one way that **technology** has changed **transportation.**

❷ **Main Idea** Name one way that people from Europe changed North America.

HANDS ON **Activity** Make a chart of how your community has changed over time. List what your community was like in the past and what it is like in the present.

Understanding the Past

Vocabulary

artifact

interview

Reading Skill

**Main Idea and
Details**

STANDARDS

CORE: 2.4.03a Good citizens; justice, truth, equality, and responsibility for the common good **2.5.01b** People and events influence local community history **2.5.03c** Interpreting time periods using photographs and interviews

EXTEND: 2.4.03c Ordinary people, good citizenship **2.5.03c** Interpreting time periods

Children from East Tennessee used these toys in the past.

Build on What You Know

What are some different ways to learn about the past?

Learning About the Past

main
(★)
idea

You can learn about the past in many ways. One way is to look at pictures or artifacts. An **artifact** is a thing that was made by people in the past. You can also read old newspapers or books about the past. An interview is another way to find out about the past. In an **interview** one person asks another person questions about a topic.

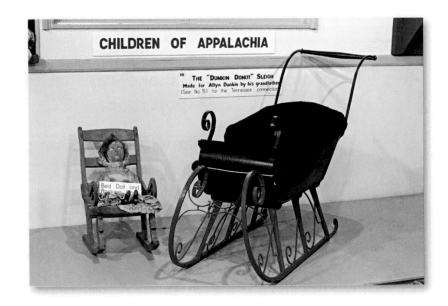

CHILDREN OF APPALACHIA

Thinking About the Past

People sometimes interpret, or think about, the past in different ways. Two people may read, see, or do the same thing in the past. But they may think about the event in different ways. Read the two different thoughts about what happened in school last week.

main idea ★

Last week was great. I went on a field trip and took one easy test.

Last week was awful. I had a really hard test.

Review What are three ways you can learn about history?

Women's Rights in Tennessee

You can learn more about different ways people think about Tennessee's past by looking at photographs, artifacts, and interviews.

Many years ago, women could not vote in the United States. Only men were allowed to vote. Some people in Tennessee thought that women should be able to vote. Others did not agree.

Lizzie Crozier French from Knoxville gave many speeches for women's right to vote.

"Home is the woman's sphere [place]."
—A Tennessean against women voting

"Women's sphere is the world."
—Catherine Tatey Kenny

What can you learn from the photos and words?

Skill **Visual Learning** Are these women for or against women's right to vote? Why do you think as you do?

Review In what way can reading people's own words tell you more about the fight for women's right to vote?

Lesson Review

1. 2.5.03c 2. 2.5.03c **Activity** 2.5.03c

❶ **Vocabulary** Write a sentence using the word **artifact.**

❷ **Main Idea** Do people always remember the past in the same way? Why or why not?

Activity Interview two people in your family to learn about something that happened in the past. Compare and contrast what the two people say about the same event.

Two Patriots

Abigail Adams and Paul Revere were patriots. Their actions showed they cared for their country.

Abigail Adams

Abigail Adams loved to write long letters. She described events in exciting detail. Letters from the past help people today to understand events long ago.

Abigail married John Adams. He was a leader in the American Revolution. He often traveled from his home in Boston. Abigail wrote to him each day. She told him about life at home. Abigail also explained her ideas about independence.

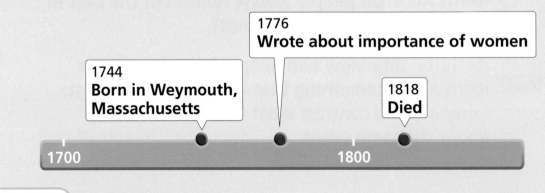

1776
Wrote about importance of women

1744
Born in Weymouth, Massachusetts

1818
Died

1700   1800

In this letter, Abigail Adams told John to "remember the ladies..." in the fight for independence.

Paul Revere

Paul Revere bravely joined other colonists who were against British rule. He did many things to fight for independence.

At night on April 18, 1775, Paul Revere rode his horse from Boston to warn colonists of a British army plan. This prepared colonists in Lexington to fight a battle that became known as the start of the American Revolution. Revere's brave ride became famous in a poem by Henry Wadsworth Longfellow.

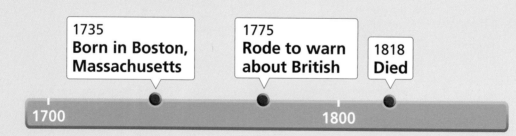

1735
Born in Boston, Massachusetts

1775
Rode to warn about British

1818
Died

1700

1800

A picture book of Longfellow's poem

Activities

1. **Tell It** Tell two ways that Paul Revere and Abigail Adams showed patriotism.

2. **Write About It** Write or tell what you might learn about the past by reading a letter from the past.

Use Reference Books

> **Vocabulary**

dictionary
encyclopedia

You can find out more about almost any topic by using reference books. A **dictionary** is a book that tells what words mean. An **encyclopedia** is a set of books that has articles on different topics. The articles tell facts.

Learn the Skill

Follow the steps below.

Step 1 The information in reference books is often in ABC order. To find the word **bank** in a dictionary, look in the section that begins with *B*. To find an article about **banks** in an encyclopedia, look in the book labeled with the letter *B*.

Step 2 After you find the *B* section, you need to find the right page. The **guide words** can help you. They show the first and last word on each page.

Step 3 Use ABC order to find the word **bank.**

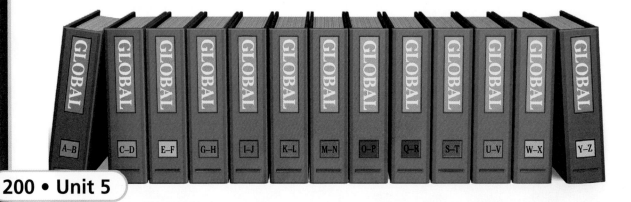

Practice the Skill

Follow the directions.

1 Suppose your teacher asks you to find information about women's rights. Tell which kind of reference book you will use.

2 Use a dictionary to find the definition of these words: **equality** and **justice**.

Guide words

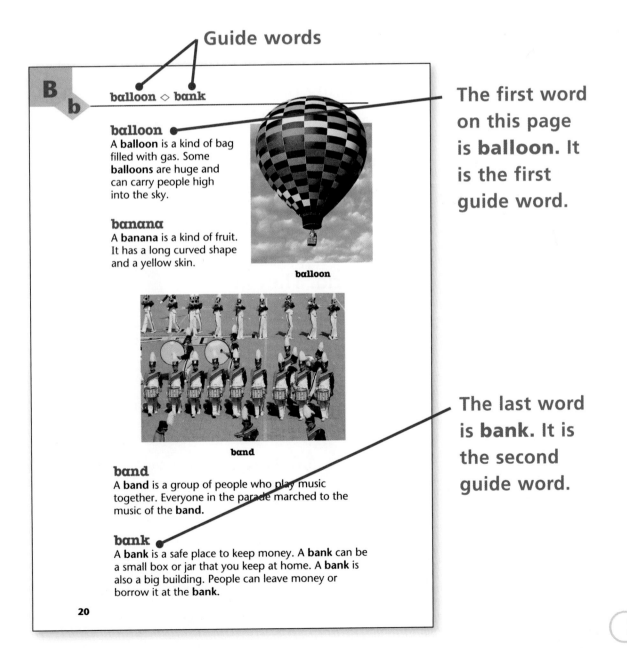

The first word on this page is **balloon.** It is the first guide word.

The last word is **bank.** It is the second guide word.

20

Tennessee Heroes

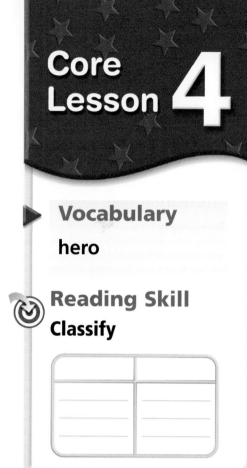

Vocabulary

hero

Reading Skill

Classify

STANDARDS

CORE: 2.4.03a Good citizenship; justice, truth, equality, and responsibility for the common good **2.5.01b** Local people and events influence community history

Build on What You Know

Think of a person you look up to. What makes that person important to you?

Heroes

Local heroes have shaped Tennessee's history. A **hero** is someone who does something brave for the good of others. A hero might also work hard to help other people. Some Tennessee heroes helped make people's lives better. They made a difference in Tennessee and around the world. They are still important today.

main idea

★ Nancy Ward ★

Nancy Ward was a Cherokee leader. She fought beside Cherokee men during a battle. After the battle, she was given the title "Beloved Woman." This honor was only given to a few brave and wise Cherokee women. <u>Ward became an important leader.</u> She tried to get justice for her people when Europeans moved onto their land. Ward worked for peace.

main idea (★)

Nancy Ward was born in what is present-day Monroe County, Tennessee. This statue of Ward is in Liberty Hill.

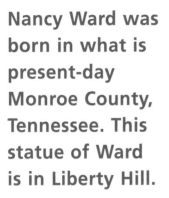

Monroe County

Review Why is Nancy Ward a hero to many people?

★ Alvin York ★

Alvin York was a hero from Pall Mall, Tennessee. He helped a small group of United States soldiers win a battle against a much larger army during World War I. York won medals from the United States and other countries for his bravery. When he came back from the war, he felt a responsibility to help others. York worked to start schools for children in rural areas of Tennessee.

Pall Mall

You can visit Alvin York's birthplace at the Sergeant Alvin C. York Historic Park in Pall Mall, Tennessee.

★ Wilma Rudolph ★

main idea

Wilma Rudolph worked hard to become a fast runner. Rudolph won three gold medals in the 1960 Olympics. When she won, most African Americans were not treated fairly in the United States. Wilma showed that when people are treated with equality, anyone can be a hero.

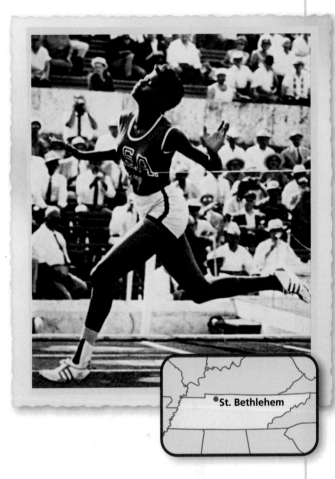

Wilma Rudolph was born in St. Bethlehem, Tennessee.

St. Bethlehem

Review In what ways were Alvin York and Wilma Rudolph alike?

Lesson Review

1. 2.4.03a **2.** 2.5.01b **Activity** 2.5.01b

❶ **Vocabulary** Write a sentence that tells why one of the people you read about is a Tennessee **hero.**

❷ **Main Idea** In what ways did these heroes shape Tennessee history?

▸ **Activity** Choose a hero in the lesson. Write or tell two things the hero could feel proud about.

Understand an Opinion

▶ **Vocabulary**

opinion

An **opinion** is what someone thinks about something. Listening to what people say can help you understand their point of view, or opinion.

Learn the Skill

Step 1 Read this question. **Which Tennessee hero do you think did the most important thing for others?**

Step 2 Read two different points of view.

- **Jeff:** I think Alvin York did the most important thing because he started schools to help children.
- **Sheera:** Wilma Rudolph did the most important thing. She showed that all people should be treated with equality.

Step 3 Jeff and Sheera gave reasons for their opinions. Tell how their opinions are different.

Practice the Skill

1 Think about the people in your life who may be heroes. Which hero in your life do you think does the most important things?

2 Give your reasons for your opinion.

3 Tell a way that your opinion is different from the opinion of someone in your class.

Nurses and doctors can be heroes.

Parents can be heroes too.

Celebrations

Vocabulary

holiday
celebration

Reading Skill
Main Idea and Details

STANDARDS
CORE: 2.5.01a Community, state, and national celebrations; Memorial Day and Independence Day

Build on What You Know

Name some holidays you know. What makes them special?

Holidays Have a History

Communities, states, and countries all have holidays. A **holiday** is a day that honors a person or an event. Holidays honor someone or something that is important to a group of people. A whole country honors national holidays on the same date.

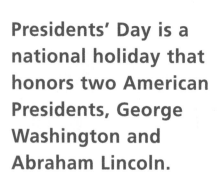

Presidents' Day is a national holiday that honors two American Presidents, George Washington and Abraham Lincoln.

Memorial Day and Independence Day are (★) main idea two national holidays in the United States. On Memorial Day, we honor all the people who died while fighting for our country. We celebrate Independence Day every year on July 4. On July 4, 1776, a group of citizens signed an important paper called the Declaration of Independence. The Declaration announced the beginning of the United States of America.

Review Why do we celebrate Memorial Day?

Every year on July 4, we celebrate the beginning of our country by having parades, picnics, and fireworks.

State Celebrations

States can have their own holidays or celebrations. A **celebration** is an event or gathering that honors someone or something. State celebrations usually honor an event, a person, or a product that is important to that state. Each year, the Tennessee State Fair celebrates Tennessee culture. The Davy Crockett Days celebration in Rutherford honors Davy Crockett.

Children win prizes at the state fair for animals they have raised by themselves.

People enjoy pig races and amusement rides at the fair.

Community Celebrations

Communities have their own celebrations. <u>Community celebrations honor someone or something that is important to the community.</u> Celebrations can include parades, music, and food. People in Pigeon Forge celebrate their culture during AppalachiaFest. McNairy County has a festival each year to honor Sheriff Buford Pusser.

Review What holidays does your community celebrate?

Every January, Memphis holds a parade to honor Dr. Martin Luther King, Jr.

Lesson Review

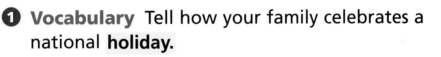

1. 2.5.01a 2. 2.5.01a **Activity** 2.5.01a

❶ **Vocabulary** Tell how your family celebrates a national **holiday.**

❷ **Main Idea** What is one way that a community celebration is different from a national celebration?

HANDS ON **Activity** Plan one way to enjoy a Tennessee state celebration.

Big Ideas · The Big Idea

Timeline in American History

| 1492 | 1607 | 1776 |

1400 — 1500 — 1600 — 1700 — 1800

American Indian communities

Explorers come from Europe

Settlers come from England

American colonists want independence

Find the missing words from the timeline.

1. _____ lived in North America before explorers came. 2.5.03b

2. Some explorers from Europe came to North America in _____. 2.5.02b

3. _____ came from England to start new communities. 2.5.03b

4. In 1776, _____ said they wanted independence. 2.5.01a

Vocabulary

Choose the letter of the word that best matches the picture.

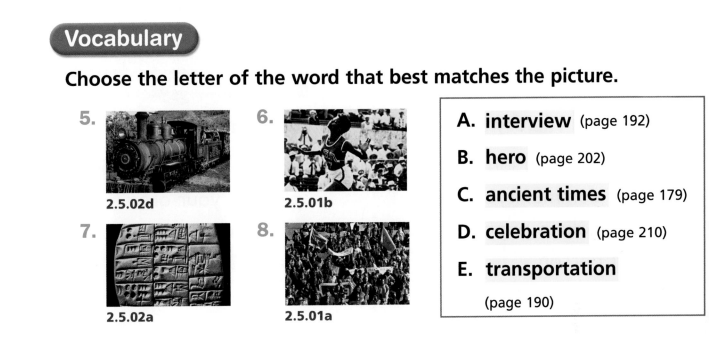

5.

2.5.02d

6.

2.5.01b

7.

2.5.02a

8.

2.5.01a

A. **interview** (page 192)

B. **hero** (page 202)

C. **ancient times** (page 179)

D. **celebration** (page 210)

E. **transportation**
(page 190)

Critical Thinking

9. Why might you learn different things about the past by talking to two different people? 2.5.03c

10. Why do you think people communicated differently in ancient times than they do in modern times? 2.5.02a, 2.5.02d

11. Name a Tennessee hero and explain what he or she did to help others. 2.4.03c, 2.5.01b

Unit Project

The Big Idea

Make a History Puppet

Choose a person from your community's history and make a puppet of that person.

❶ Make the puppet's head and costume.

❷ Write three questions that you would like people to ask your puppet.

❸ Use your hand and voice so that your puppet answers the questions.

2.5.01b

CURRENT EVENTS
WEEKLY (WR) READER

Current Events Project

What events are taking place in your area? Make an **Events in the News Timeline.**

MONUMENT TIMELINE

2004	2005	2006	2007	2008

February 2004
Monument
planned

June 2006
Building
begins

October 2008
Monument
done

2.5.03b

Technology

Read articles about current events at www.eduplace.com/kids/hmss/

Directions

Use the timeline below and what you know to do Numbers 12 and 13.

Dan's Life History

| 0 | 1 | 2 | 3 | 4 | 5 | 6 | 7 | 8 | 9 |

Dan was born.   Dan learned to read.   _____

12 Which of these is the **best** label for the last picture on the timeline?   2.5.03b

(A) Dan today.

(F) Dan wrote a book.

(C) Dan learned to read.

(D) Dan learned to juggle.

13 How old is Dan today?   2.5.03b

(A) 8 years old

(F) 1 year old

(C) 6 years old

(D) 4 years old

Veterans Day

Veterans Day honors people who were in the army and other armed forces. Soldiers, sailors, and pilots who served the United States are veterans.

Many veterans march in Veterans Day parades. People thank our veterans for helping our country when it is at war and at peace.

A Purple Heart medal

Activity

Thank-You Letter

1. Write a thank-you letter to a veteran.

2. You may display your letter or mail it to a group of veterans.

Dear Veterans,
Thank you for fighting for the United States. Our country is safe because of your work.
Sincerely,
Roberto Gonzalez

STANDARDS
2.5.01a Celebrations

Thanksgiving

On Thanksgiving Day people give thanks for what they have. This tradition began long ago when Pilgrims shared their first harvest with the Wampanoag.

In 1863, President Abraham Lincoln thought the United States should have a day of thanks. He started the national holiday we celebrate today.

American families of many backgrounds celebrate Thanksgiving Day. People may eat foods from their own culture. They may eat turkey and cranberry sauce too. Many families talk about why they feel thankful on Thanksgiving.

Activity

Thanksgiving Stick Puppets

1. Make stick puppets of the Pilgrims and the Wampanoag.

2. What do you think the Pilgrims and the Wampanoag felt thankful for? Use the puppets to act out your ideas.

STANDARDS
2.5.01a Celebrations

217

Martin Luther King, Jr. Day

Dr. Martin Luther King, Jr., worked to make fair laws for all people. Each year, people in the United States honor his work.

Dr. King knew that some laws were not fair to African Americans. He gave speeches and marched to show the need to change the unfair laws. He shared his dream of equal rights for all. He received the Nobel Peace Prize for his work.

Activity

Dream Doves

1. Think of a dream that you believe is good for everyone.

2. Write your dream on the shape of a dove.

• peace

• friendship

• happiness

Presidents' Day

On Presidents' Day, people honor two important Presidents of the United States.

George Washington helped make the United States a free country. He led an army for the new country in the American Revolution. He was the first President of the United States.

Abraham Lincoln was another great President.

He helped make all people in the United States equal and free. Lincoln helped keep the states together in one country.

Activity

"If I Am President" Poster

1. Think about what you would do if you were the President of the United States.

2. Make a poster to show your ideas.

Jenny for President !!!
I will:
plant trees
clean up trash
give children books

STANDARDS
2.4.03a Equality, responsibility
2.5.01a Celebrations

Memorial Day

Vietnam Veterans Memorial

On Memorial Day, citizens of the United States remember the people who fought and died in wars.

A memorial is something that helps people remember a person, a group, or an event from the past. A memorial can be a statue, a sign, or a building. On Memorial Day, people put flowers and flags on memorials and graves. Towns and cities have parades or speeches. Citizens honor the people who fought for the United States.

Activity

Make a Memorial Circle

1. Think of a person or an event you want to remember.

2. Write the words on a circle of colored paper. You may add a picture.

In memory of my grandpa Ted Barrios

In memory of people who fought in all wars

STANDARDS
2.5.01a Celebrations, Memorial Day

Flag Day

The United States flag is a symbol for our country. On Flag Day, many communities have parades and sing the national anthem.

Our country's first flag had only 13 stripes and 13 stars. They stood for the 13 colonies that formed our country. Later the colonies became states.

Now there are 50 states in the United States. The United States flag has 50 stars that stand for our 50 states. It still has 13 stripes.

Activity

State Stars

1. Cut out the shape of a white star.

2. Write the name of a state in red. Write the capital of the state in blue.

STANDARDS
2.4.04c Patriotic symbols
2.5.01a Celebrations

Independence Day

On the Fourth of July, we celebrate our country's birthday.

On July 4, 1776, our leaders signed the Declaration of Independence. It said that our land and our people were now free from Great Britain.

Independence is another word for **freedom.** Every Fourth of July, we celebrate our country's freedom. Towns and cities have parades and picnics. Many communities have fireworks at night.

Activity

Freedom Poem

1. Think of some things that United States citizens are free to do.

2. Write a poem about your freedoms. You may start with the words "I am free . . ."

I am free to read books and talk to people.

I am free to think and learn.

I am free to be me!

References

Citizenship Handbook

Resources

Our Flag

Pledge of Allegiance

I **pledge allegiance** to the flag
of the United States of America
and to the **Republic** for which it stands,
one Nation under God, **indivisible,**
with **liberty** and **justice** for all.

**What does the Pledge of Allegiance mean?
Use the vocabulary to explain.**

pledge: promise
allegiance: loyalty
republic: nation
indivisible: cannot be divided
liberty: freedom
justice: fairness

Rules about the Flag

Look at some rules about our national flag. They come from a law called the United States Flag Code.

- The flag should have thirteen stripes, red and white. It should have white stars on a blue background. It should have a star for each state.

- To salute the flag, stand straight and face the flag. Put your right hand on your heart.

- Say the pledge while you salute.

- Do not let the flag touch the ground.

- Fly the United States flag above any state flag.

- At night, take down the flag or light it up.

Character Traits

A **character trait** is something people show by the way they act. A person who acts bravely shows courage. Courage is a character trait.

Character traits are also called "life skills." Life skills can help you do your best. Doing your best helps you reach your goals.

Coretta Scott King
Courage
Coretta Scott King showed courage by speaking out for the rights of African Americans.

Paul Revere
Patriotism
Paul Revere showed patriotism by warning the colonists about the plans of the British army.

Courage means acting bravely. It takes courage to be honest and tell the truth.

Patriotism is being proud of your country and working for your country's goals.

Responsibility means doing all your work. You can count on people who show responsibility. They will do all the things they are asked to do.

Respect means paying attention to what other people want and believe. Treating others with respect helps everyone get along.

Fairness means acting to make things fair for everyone. People can work for justice and equality for all people.

Civic virtue is good citizenship. It means telling the truth and doing things to help people live and work well together.

Caring is helping others. Listening to how other people feel is also caring.

Atlas

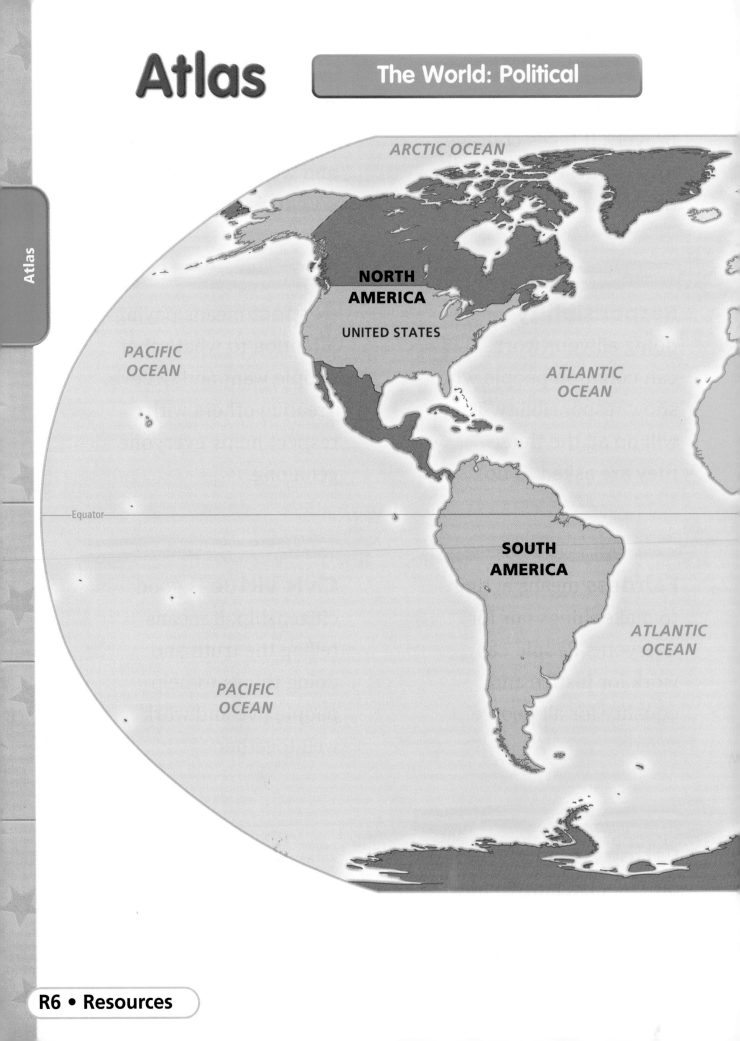

ARCTIC OCEAN

NORTH
AMERICA

UNITED STATES

PACIFIC
OCEAN

ATLANTIC
OCEAN

Equator

SOUTH
AMERICA

ATLANTIC
OCEAN

PACIFIC
OCEAN

Atlas

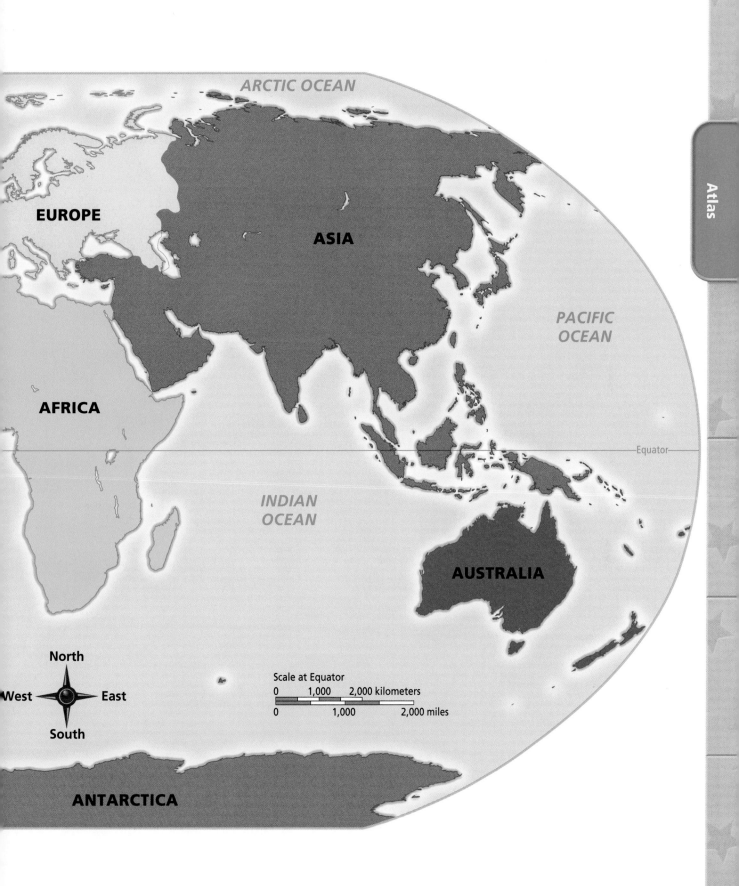

ARCTIC OCEAN

EUROPE

ASIA

PACIFIC
OCEAN

AFRICA

Equator

INDIAN
OCEAN

AUSTRALIA

North

West   East

South

ANTARCTICA

Scale at Equator
0   1,000   2,000 kilometers

0   1,000   2,000 miles

Atlas

North
West · East
South

PACIFIC OCEAN

Map Key

⊛ National Capital

— National Boundary

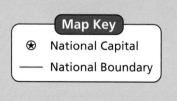

0	400	800 kilometers
0	400	800 miles

ARCTIC OCEAN

CANADA

Ottawa ⍟

UNITED STATES

Washington, D.C. ⍟

ATLANTIC OCEAN

MEXICO

Mexico City ⍟

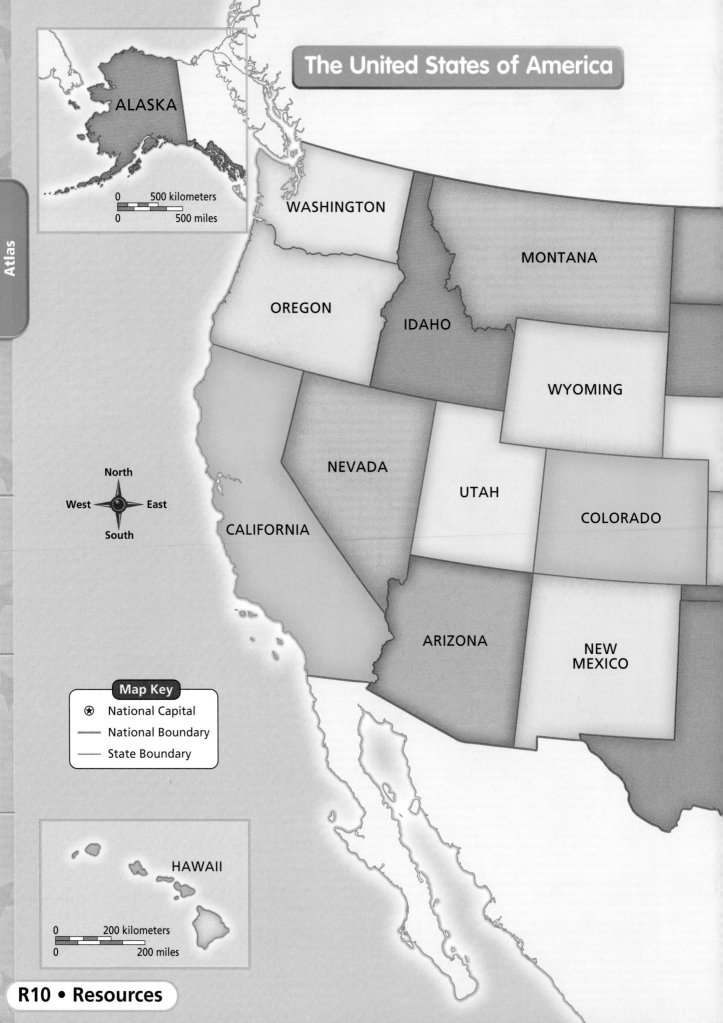

The United States of America

ALASKA

0   500 kilometers
0   500 miles

Atlas

WASHINGTON

OREGON

IDAHO

MONTANA

WYOMING

North

West   East

South

NEVADA

UTAH

COLORADO

CALIFORNIA

ARIZONA

NEW MEXICO

Map Key

⊛   National Capital

───   National Boundary

───   State Boundary

HAWAII

0   200 kilometers
0   200 miles

NEW
HAMPSHIRE

VERMONT

MAINE

MASSACHUSETTS

NORTH
DAKOTA

MINNESOTA

SOUTH
DAKOTA

WISCONSIN

MICHIGAN

NEW
YORK

RHODE
ISLAND

CONNECTICUT

PENNSYLVANIA

NEW
JERSEY

NEBRASKA

IOWA

ILLINOIS

INDIANA

OHIO

WEST
VIRGINIA

DELAWARE

Washington, D.C.

MARYLAND

VIRGINIA

KANSAS

MISSOURI

KENTUCKY

NORTH
CAROLINA

TENNESSEE

OKLAHOMA

ARKANSAS

SOUTH
CAROLINA

ALABAMA

GEORGIA

MISSISSIPPI

TEXAS

LOUISIANA

FLORIDA

0   125   250 kilometers

0   125   250 miles

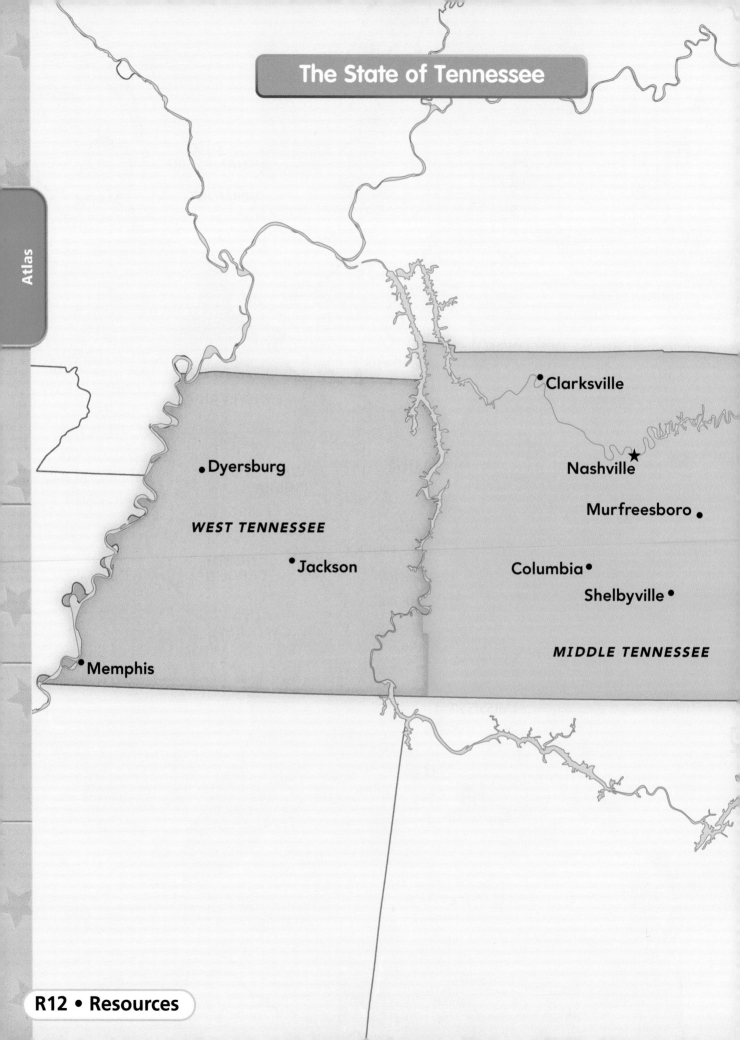

The State of Tennessee

Atlas

- Clarksville
- Dyersburg
- Nashville ★
- **WEST TENNESSEE**
- Murfreesboro
- Jackson
- Columbia
- Shelbyville
- **MIDDLE TENNESSEE**
- Memphis

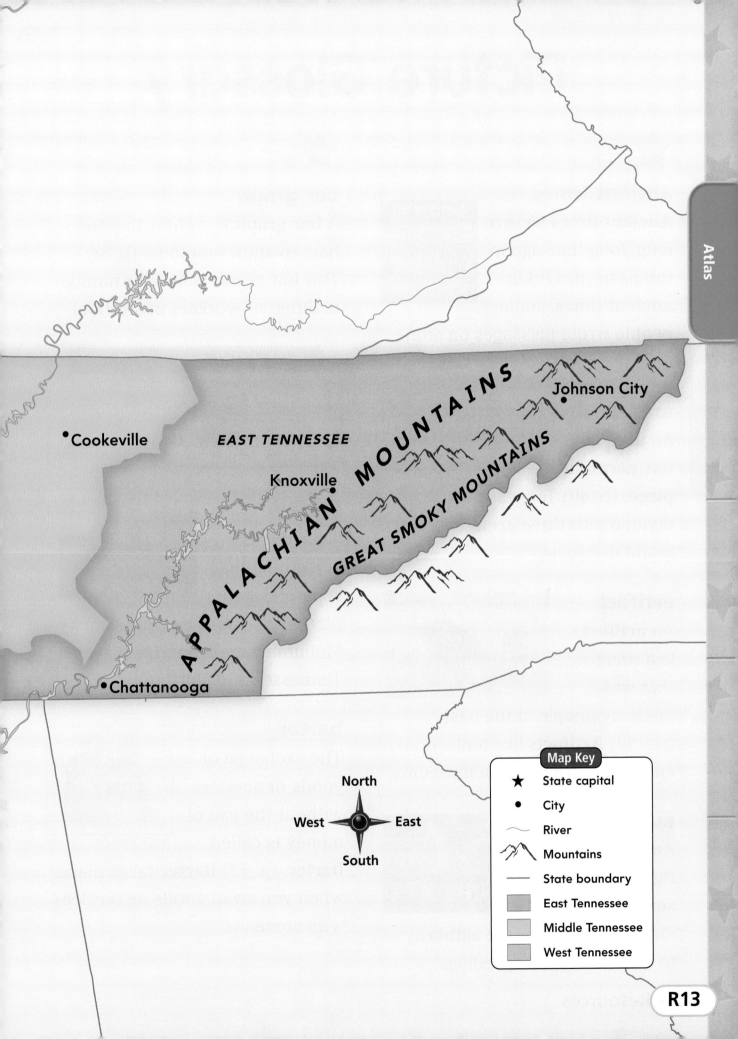

APPALACHIAN MOUNTAINS

EAST TENNESSEE

GREAT SMOKY MOUNTAINS

•Cookeville

Johnson City

Knoxville•

•Chattanooga

North

West ✦ East

South

Map Key

★ State capital

• City

～ River

⛰ Mountains

— State boundary

▢ East Tennessee

▢ Middle Tennessee

▢ West Tennessee

Picture Glossary

A

ancient times

Ancient times were a long, long time ago in the past. (p. 179) In **ancient times,** some people wrote messages on stone or clay.

area

An **area** is one part of a place. (p. 40) Tennessee is divided into three **areas** called grand divisions.

artifact

An **artifact** is a thing that was made by people in the past. (p. 192) **Artifacts** like tools, dolls, and books are found in museums.

authority

Authority is the right to do something. (p. 154) Police officers have the **authority** to write tickets for speeding.

B

bar graph

A **bar graph** is a chart that uses bars to show amounts. (p. 58) This **bar graph** shows the number of different workers in a school.

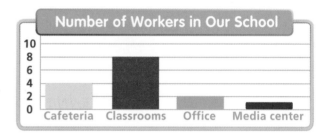

Number of Workers in Our School

Cafeteria   Classrooms   Office   Media center

barrier

A **barrier** is something that separates two places. (p. 108) The Great Smoky Mountains are a **barrier** between Tennessee and North Carolina.

barter

The exchange of goods or services without the use of money is called **barter.** (p. 72) **Barter** takes place when you swap goods or services with someone.

C

calendar

A **calendar** is a chart that shows the months, weeks, and days of the year. (p. 32) I marked my birthday on the **calendar.**

capital

A **capital** is a city where the people in a government work. (p. 138) The **capital** of Tennessee is Nashville.

capital resource

A **capital resource** is something other than natural or human resources that people need in order to make and move goods. (p. 69) **Capital resources** include tools, machinery, buildings, and trucks.

cardinal directions

The **cardinal directions** are north, south, east, and west. (p. 44) A compass rose shows the **cardinal directions** on a map.

cause

A **cause** is something that makes something else happen. (p. 150) The **cause** of the fire was a lightning strike.

celebration

A **celebration** is an event or a gathering that honors someone or something. (p. 210) Many cities hold **celebrations** to honor Dr. Martin Luther King, Jr.

chronology

Chronology is the order in which things happen. (p. 178) Understanding **chronology** helps you learn about history.

citizen

A **citizen** is a person who belongs to a place. (p. 142) You are a **citizen** of the community where you live.

city

A **city** is a place where many people live and work (p. 96) Nashville is an important **city** in Tennessee.

climate

The usual weather of a place over a long time is called **climate.** (p. 123) Southern Michigan has a **climate** with cold winters and warm summers.

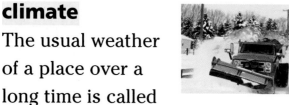

community

A **community** is a place where people live, play, and work together. (p. 35) Cities and towns are **communities.**

compass rose

A **compass rose** is a drawing that shows directions on a map. (p. 24) Use the **compass rose** to find north.

consumer

A **consumer** is someone who buys or uses goods or services. (p. 60) I am a **consumer** when I buy food at a store.

continent

A **continent** is a large body of land. (p. 90) Earth has seven **continents.**

country

A **country** is a part of the world with its own leaders and rules. (p. 34) Mexico is the **country** south of the United States.

culture

The way of life of a group of people is called **culture.** (p. 19) Religious beliefs are part of people's **culture.**

custom

A **custom** is something that people usually do at a certain time. (p. 19) It is our **custom** to wear party hats at birthday parties.

decision

A **decision** is the act of deciding or of making a choice. (p. 162) I had to make a **decision** about doing my homework before or after supper.

detail

A **detail** is a small piece of information. (p. 116) Make sure you support your idea with **details.**

Main Idea
Details
1.
2.
3.
4.
5.

dictionary

A **dictionary** is a book that tells what words mean. (p. 200) Look up new words in a **dictionary.**

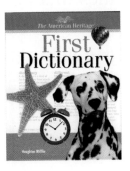

distance

The word **distance** means how far one point is from another. (p. 78) The **distance** across the table is 30 inches.

duty

A **duty** is something a person should do. (p. 153) You have a **duty** to follow the laws in your community.

effect

An **effect** is something that happens as a result of a cause. (p. 150) An **effect** of playing in puddles is wet clothing.

cause → effect

election

An **election** is a time when people vote. (p. 158) We have an **election** to choose a new President every four years.

encyclopedia

An **encyclopedia** is a set of books that has articles about many topics. (p. 200) Look up a topic in an **encyclopedia** to find out more about it.

environment

The **environment** is the natural world around you. (p. 121) Land, water, plants, animals, and people are all part of the **environment.**

Equator

The **Equator** is an imaginary line that divides Earth into its northern and southern halves. (p. 94) You can only see the **Equator** on maps and globes.

export

Export means to send things to another country. (p. 74) Tennessee **exports** car parts, cotton, and country music.

globe

A **globe** is a ball-shaped model of Earth. (p. 22) A **globe** shows the true shape of Earth.

goods

Things people make or grow are called **goods.** (p. 56) Trucks and apples are two types of **goods.**

government

A group of people who work together to run a community, state, or country make up a **government.** (p. 136) Some people in our **government** work at city hall.

grid

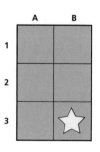

A **grid** is a pattern of lines that form boxes. (p. 102) A **grid** helps you find places on a map.

hemisphere

A **hemisphere** is half of Earth. (p. 94) North America is in the Western **Hemisphere.**

heritage

Heritage is all the important traditions that are passed down in families and communities. (p. 42) Davy Crockett's statue tells about Tennessee's **heritage.**

hero

A **hero** is someone who does something brave for the good of others or works hard to help others. (p. 202) **Heroes** can be found in areas such as medicine, sports, and science.

history

Everything people can know about the past is called **history.** (p. 180) The invention of the computer was an important event in **history.**

holiday

A **holiday** is a special day that honors a person or an event. (p. 208) Independence Day is a **holiday** that honors the creation of the United States of America.

human resource

A **human resource** is a person who helps produce goods or services. (p. 69) A worker in a factory or other places is a **human resource.**

immigrant

An **immigrant** is a person who moves from one country to another. (p. 34) In the 1970s, many **immigrants** came to the United States from Asia.

import

Import means to bring things into a country from another country. (p. 74) The United States **imports** oil for its many industries.

income

The money people earn when they work is called **income.** (p. 54) My mother uses her **income** to pay for our food.

industry

An **industry** is a group of businesses that produce or make something. (p. 68) Farming is an important **industry** in Tennessee.

intermediate directions

Intermediate directions are directions that fall between the cardinal directions of north, south, east, and west. (p. 44) Northwest, northeast, southeast, and southwest are **intermediate directions.**

interview

An **interview** is a meeting in which one person asks another person questions about a topic. (p. 192) We asked five questions during our **interview** with the mayor.

justice

Justice means fairness. (p. 145) A good judge treats everyone with **justice.**

lake

A body of water with land all around it is called a **lake.** (p. 106) Most **lakes** have fresh water.

landform

A **landform** is one of the shapes of land found on the earth. (p. 104) A mountain is a **landform.**

landmark

A **landmark** is something that helps people know a place. (pp. 42, 176) The Hermitage is a **landmark** in Tennessee.

law

A rule that everyone in a community, state, or country must follow is called a **law.** (p. 152) A driver who doesn't stop at a stop sign breaks the **law.**

legend

A **legend** is a story that has been told for years and years. (p. 28) Many cultures have **legends** about animals.

location

A **location** is a place. (p. 102) An airplane symbol may mark the **location** of an airport on a map.

loyalty

Loyalty is a strong feeling of support for a person or a place. (p. 40) Many Tennesseans feel **loyalty** to their grand division.

main idea

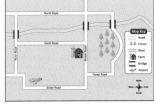

The most important thought in a paragraph is called a **main idea.** (p. 116) The **main idea** on that page is that people have many kinds of pets.

map

A **map** is a flat drawing of a place as seen from above. (p. 22) A **map** tells you how to find different places.

mineral

A **mineral** is something from nature that is not a plant or an animal. (p. 118) Coal and limestone are two **minerals** found in Tennessee.

modern times

Modern times are now and just a few years in the past. (p. 179) In **modern times,** people can communicate using computers.

monument

A **monument** is something that honors a hero or an event. (p. 168) Many towns have a **monument** to people who served in a war.

nation

Nation is another word for country. (p. 91) Canada is a **nation** to the north of the United States.

natural resource

Something in nature that people use is a **natural resource.** (p. 69) Water is an important **natural resource.**

opinion

An **opinion** is what someone thinks about something. (p. 206) We each had a different **opinion** about which play to put on.

pole

The place on Earth that is farthest north or south is a kind of **pole.** (p. 94) The North **Pole** and the South **Pole** are very cold.

privilege

A **privilege** is another word for a right. (p. 161) Citizens over 18 in the United States have the **privilege** of voting.

producer

A **producer** is a person who makes or grows goods. (p. 60) A baker is a **producer** of bread and rolls.

qualification

A **qualification** is a skill that makes a person good for a job. (p. 160) Citizens should choose a leader with the best **qualifications.**

region

A **region** is an area that has a shared natural or human feature that sets it apart from other areas. (p. 112) The state of Tennessee is divided into three **regions.**

right

A **right** is something you are allowed to do by law. (p. 142) You have the **right** to speak freely.

river

A **river** is a long, moving body of fresh water. (p. 107) The Mississippi River is an important **river** in Tennessee.

rural area

A **rural area** is a place that has more open space, but fewer buildings than a city or suburb has. (p. 100) Farms are found in **rural areas.**

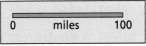

scale

A line with a series of marks used to find distance on a map is a **scale.** (p. 78) Use a map **scale** to find how far apart two places are.

services

Activities that people do to help other people are called **services.** (p. 57) Dentists provide **services.**

settlement

A **settlement** is a small community started by people from another place. (p. 187) Europeans created the **settlement** of Plymouth in North America.

specialized worker

A **specialized worker** is a person who does just one main job. (p. 64) **Specialized workers** in Costa Rica grow bananas.

state

Part of a country is called a **state.** (p. 89) Tennessee is one **state** in the United States.

TENNESSEE

suburb

A **suburb** is a community near a city. (p. 99) Many people who live in **suburbs** work in nearby cities.

symbol

A **symbol** is a picture, place, or thing that stands for something else. (pp. 24, 164) An eagle is a **symbol** of freedom.

taxes

Taxes are money that a government collects from citizens and businesses. (p. 141) Local governments use money from **taxes** to pay for services such as police.

Baseball Bat 35.00
Baseball 8.00
Baseball glove 40.00

SUBTOTAL 83.00
Tennessee Tax 7.00% 5.81
TOTAL $88.81

Cash 90.00
Cash Change 1.19

technology

The use of science to make things work better is called **technology.** (p. 191) People use **technology** to make safer cars.

tilt

Tilt means to lean to one side. (p. 126) Earth has a **tilt** toward the sun and away from the sun at different times of year.

timeline

A **timeline** is an ordered group of words and dates that show when events happened. (p. 184) A **timeline** can tell about your life.

Dan's Life History
0 1 2 3 4 5 6 7 8 9
Dan was born   Dan learned to read   Dan today

trade

The buying and selling of goods and services is called **trade.** (p. 73) People take part in **trade** in many ways.

LEMONADE 25

tradition

A **tradition** is an idea or custom that  is passed down in a family. (p. 26) One **tradition** in my family is that we eat turkey on Thanksgiving Day.

transportation

Any way of moving things or people from  one place to another is called **transportation.** (p. 190) Cars are one kind of **transportation.**

urban area

Urban area is another name for city. (p. 98) An  **urban area** has many buildings and people.

valley

 The low land between mountains or hills is called a **valley.** (p. 105) A **valley** often has a river running through it.

vegetation

Vegetation means all the plants that grow naturally in an area.  (p. 114) Tennessee's **vegetation** includes trees that can grow in the Smoky Mountains.

volunteer

A **volunteer** does a job without being  paid. (p. 143) A **volunteer** might help collect food for others.

vote

To **vote** means to show or write a choice for a leader or a law.  (p. 158) You may **vote** for class president or team captain.

weather

What the air is like outside at any given time is called **weather.** (p. 122) Today the **weather** is warm and rainy.

Index

Page numbers with m after them refer to maps.

Acknowledgments

For each of the selections listed below, grateful acknowledgement is made for permission to excerpt and/or reprint original or copyrighted material, as follows:

Permissioned Text

Lyrics from "I Live in a City," words and music by Malvina Reynolds. Copyright ©1961 by Schroder Music Co. (ASCAP) Renewed 1989. Used by permission. All rights reserved.

Excerpt from "Our Family Comes From 'Round the World," from *Fathers, Mothers, Sisters, Brothers,* by Mary Ann Hoberman. Copyright ©1991 by Mary Ann Hoberman. Reprinted by permission of Little, Brown, and Company, (Ind.) and Gina Maccoby Literary Agency.

Excerpt from "Wouth" ("The Great Smokies"), from *Between Earth & Sky: Legends of Native American Sacred Places,* by Joseph Bruchac. Copyright ©1996 by Joseph Bruchac. Reprinted by permission of Harcourt, Inc. and Barbara S. Kouts Agency.

93 Tamara Jernigan quotation taken from: Lawrence Livermore National Laboratory Public Affairs Office. "Livermore Lab Astronaut to Highlight Space Shuttle Missions." News Release (March 17, 2003). http://www.llnl.gov/pao/news/news_releases/2003/NR-03-03-07.html

Illustrations

30 Steve Harrington. **62, 63** CA Nobens. **66** Len Ebert. **112–3** Michael Maydak. **151** Michelle Gengaro. **152, R21** Ron Berg. **R18** Peter Richardson.

Maps

Maps by Maps.com

Photography

4 Arthur Tilly/Taxi/Getty Images. **5–6** ©AGStockUSA, Inc./Alamy. **7** ©Dennis MacDonald/PhotoEdit. **8** ©Underwood & Underwood/CORBIS. **12** ©Ariel Skelley/Getty Images. **13** National Portrait Gallery, Smithsonian Institution, Washington, DC/Art Resource, NY. **14–5** Banana Stock. **16–7** (b) ©Paul Barton/CORBIS. **16** (cl) ©HMCo./Ken Karp. **17** ©Dave G. Houser/CORBIS. **18** Arthur Tilly/Taxi/Getty Images. (cr) Tony Freeman/PhotoEdit. **19** ©Jose Luis Pelaez, Inc./CORBIS. **20** ©HMCo./Ken Karp. **21** (c) Index Stock. **26** David Young-Wolff/PhotoEdit. **27** Dick Doub/Museum of Appalachia. **28** ©HMCo./Ken Karp. **29** U.S. Naval Academy Alumni Association & Foundation. **35** (bl) Lawrence Migdale. (br) Rudi Von Briel/Index Stock Imagery, Inc. **36** Knoxville Tourism & Sports Collection. **37** ©Raymond Gehman/CORBIS. **38** (bl) Courtesy of Debbie Jenkins. (br) Courtesy of the Chucalissa Museum, the University of Memphis. **39** Department of Tourist Development News Bureau. **41** (br) ©David R. Frazier Photolibrary, Inc./Alamy. (bc) AP / Wide World Photos. (bl) ©Scott Wintrow/Getty Images. **42** (bl) ©Roman Soumar/CORBIS. (br) ©Dave Bartruff/CORBIS. **43** ©Dave G. Houser/CORBIS. **50–1** David Young-Wolff/PhotoEdit. **52** Thinkstock/Getty Images. **53** (cl) ©Bob Sacha/CORBIS. (cr) ©LWA-Dann Tardif/CORBIS. **54** ©Jose Luis Pelaez, Inc./CORBIS. **55** (tr) Ed Lallo/Index Stock Imagery Inc. (bl) ©Raymond Gehman/CORBIS. **56** ©Ted Thai/Time Life Pictures/Getty Images. **57** ©CORBIS. **60** Photodisc/Getty Images. **61** ©LWA-Dann Tardif/CORBIS. **64** ©AGStockUSA, Inc./Alamy. **65** (tl) ©Royalty-Free/CORBIS. (tr) ©Asia Images Group/Alamy. **68** ©Phillip Gould/CORBIS. **69** (bc) ©Raymond Gehman/CORBIS. (bl) ©Gary Braasch/CORBIS. (br) ©Robert McGouey/Alamy. **71** ©Ed Eckstein/CORBIS.

72 Lisa Campbell Ernst. **73** (bl) Allan Davey/Masterfile. (br) Taxi/Getty Images **75** (cl) ©Keith Wood/CORBIS. (cr) ©Reuters/CORBIS. **84–5** ©Donna Ikenberry/Animals Animals-Earth Scenes. **86** Gibson Stock Photography. **87** (cl) © Londie G Padelsky/Panoramic Images. (cr) Dan Budnik/Woodfin Camp & Associates. **88** ©HMCo./Ken Karp. **89** ©HMCo./Ken Karp. **92** Image produced by F. Hasler, M. Jentoft-Nilsen, H. Pierce, K. Palaniappan and M. Manyin. NASA Goddard Lab for Atmospheres—data from National Oceanic and Atmospheric Administration. **93** ©CORBIS. **96** ©Richard Cummins/SuperStock. **98** Mark Segal/Panoramic Images. **99** AP / Wide World Photos. **100** ©Rob Harling/Alamy. **104** © Londie G Padelsky/Panoramic Images. **105** ©Patrick Bennett/CORBIS. **106** Courtesy of Nancy Moore at the Blue Basin Cove Bed & Breakfast. **107** Jim Wark/AirPhoto. **108** ©Charles E. Rotkin/CORBIS. **109** Jim Wark/AirPhoto. **110–1** (b) Donovan Reese/Panoramic Images. **111** (tr) ABPL Image Library/Animals Animals/Earth Scenes. **114** C.C. Lockwood/Bruce Coleman. **115** (tl) New Moon/Panoramic Images. (tr) Richard I'Anson/Lonely Planet images. **118** International Stock/Imagestate. **120** (bl) R. Ian Lloyd/Masterfile. (br) ©Joe Sohm/The Image Works. **121** ©Tom Brakefield/Getty Images. **124** Loni Duka/IndexStock. **125** Brad Wrobleski/Masterfile. **132–3** Ariel Skelley/Masterfile. **134** (cl) Courtesy of the Chattanooga City Council. **134–5** (b) Getty Images. **135** (cl) Courtesy of The Chattanooga Police Department, (cr) ©age fotostock/SuperStock. **136** Courtesy of the Chattanooga City Council. **137** Courtesy of the Town of Farragut. **138** ©HMCo./Angela Coppola. **140** (br) IndexStock Imagery. (cr) ©Elena Rooraid/PhotoEdit. **141** ©HMCo./Angela Coppola. **142** ©HMCo./Angela Coppola. **143** (cl) The Greater Boston Food Bank. (tr) Mark E. Gibson Color Photography. **144** (cl) Shelby County Circuit Court Judges. (br) Pierre Tremblay/Masterfile. **145** ©D. Hurst/Alamy. **147** ©HMCo./Angela Coppola. **148** ©HMCo./Angela Coppola. **153** (tr) ©Visions of America, LLC/Alamy. (tl) ©David Young-Wolff/PhotoEdit. **154** AP / Wide World Photos. **155** (cr) ©John Neubauer/PhotoEdit. (cl) Courtesy of The Chattanooga Police Department. **156** (tr) ©Reuters NewMedia Inc./CORBIS. **156–7** (b) ©Bettmann/CORBIS. **158** (b) HMCo./Jade Albert. **159** (tr) Shelbyville Times-Gazette. (cr) Governor Phil Bredesen's Photo Gallery/State of Tennessee. (br) Bell/Folio Inc. **160** (c) Steven Begleiter/Image State. (cr) Jim and Mary Whitmer. **161** AP / Wide World Photos. **163** (cl) ©Brad Wilson/Getty Images. (cr) ©Thomas Northcut/Getty Images. **164** (b) SuperStock, Inc. **164–5** (t) Ken Davies/Masterfile. **165** (br) ©Thinkstock/Getty Images. **166** (t) One Mile Up, Inc. (bl) ©Mike Briner/Alamy. **167** ©Stockbyte/CORBIS. (br) ©Coinery/Alamy. (bl) ©DLILLC/Corbis. **168** (br) ©age fotostock/SuperStock. (cl) ©Andre Jenny/Alamy. **169** ©Dennis MacDonald/PhotoEdit. **174–5** ©Jeff Greenberg/PhotoEdit. **176** (cl) ©Gianni Dagli Orti/CORBIS. (cr) H.P. Merten/Zefa/Masterfile. **177** (cl) Dick Doub/Museum of Appalachia. (cr) AP / Wide World Photos. **179** (br) ©PictureNet Corporation/Alamy. (bl) ©Gianni Dagli Orti/CORBIS. **180** YVA Momatiuk & John Eastcott/Woodfin Camp & Associates. **182–3** (all) Richard Cummins/Lonely Planet Images. **183** (c) ©CORBIS. **184** (tr) ©Myrleen Ferguson Cate/PhotoEdit. (br) Burke/Triolo/Retrofile. **185** (bl) ©Horace Bristol/CORBIS. (bc) ©Claudia Kunin/CORBIS. (br) ©Don Mason/CORBIS. **186** ©Shelly Katz/Time Life Pictures/Getty Images. **188** Lewis W. Hine/National Archives and Records Administration. **190** (cl) Underwood Photo Archives. (cr) ©Minnesota Historical Society/CORBIS. **191** (cr) ©Jeff Greenberg/PhotoEdit. (cl) ©Underwood & Underwood/CORBIS. **192** Dick

Doub/Museum of Appalachia. **193** ©HMCo./Ken Karp. **194** McClung Historical Collection. **195** Chattanooga Regional History Museum. **196** PhotoEdit. **197** Massachusetts Historical Society. **198** ©Freelance Photography Guild/CORBIS. **199** ©Rick Friedman/CORBIS. **201** (cr) ©HMCo. (b) ©HMCo. **202** ©HMCo./Ken Karp. **203** David Ray Smith/http://SmithDRay.tripod.com/nancyward-index-5.html. **204** AP / Wide World Photos. **205** ©Bettmann/CORBIS. **206** (b) ©HMCo./Ken Karp. (bc) AP / Wide World Photos. (br) ©Bettmann/CORBIS. **207** ©Chuck Savage/CORBIS. **208** (bl) ©Francis G. Mayer/CORBIS. (br) ©CORBIS. **209** ©Kevin Fleming/CORBIS. **210** (bl) Courtesy of The Tennessee State Fair. (cr) Brent Moore. **211** AP / Wide World Photos. **212** (cl) British Museum London/Art Resource. (c) ©Bettmann/CORBIS. (c) ©Richard T. Nowitz/CORBIS. (cr) ©Joseph Sohm/CORBIS. **213** (tl) Colin Garratt; Milepost. (cl) ©Gianni Dagli Orti/CORBIS. (tc) ©Bettmann/CORBIS. (c) AP / Wide World Photos. **215** (tl) ©Jim Craigmyle/CORBIS. (tc) ©Bob Thomas/Stone/Getty Images. (tr) ImageState Pictor/PictureQuest. **216** (tl) Mark Gibson Stock Photography. (c) ©Davies and Starr/The Image Bank/Getty Images. **217** ©Ronnie Kaufman/CORBIS. **218** (tl) ©Hulton-Deutsch Collection/CORBIS. (cl) ©The Nobel Foundation. **219** (tl) The Granger Collection, New York. (cr) ©CORBIS. (br) ©HMCo./Jade Albert. **220** ©Phillip James Corwin/CORBIS. **221** ©Stone/Getty Images. **222** ©Maroon/Folio, Inc. **R1** ©CORBIS. **R2** ©Elise Lewin/Photographer's Choice/Getty Images. **R3** (tr) ©Bruce Burkhart/CORBIS. (bl) ©Annie Griffiths Belt/CORBIS. (bc) ©AFP/CORBIS. (br) ©Mark Thiessen/CORBIS. **R4** (cl) ©Bettmann/CORBIS. (br) ©Arnold Michaelis/Pix Inc. **R14** (tc) ©Gianni Dagli Orti/CORBIS. (cl) Dick Doub/Museum of Appalachia. (bl) Courtesy of The Chattanooga Police Department. (cr) ©Londie G Padelsky/Panoramic Images. **R15** (cl) ©Raymond Gehman/CORBIS. (br) ©Tom & Dee Ann McCarthy/CORBIS. (cr) AP / Wide World Photos. **R16** (tl) Mark Segal/Panoramic Images. (cl) ©Photodisc/Getty Images. (bl) ©Owaki-Kulla/CORBIS. (cl) ©HMCo./Ken Karp. (br) ©Ariel Skelley/CORBIS. **R17** (tl) ©Tony Freeman/PhotoEdit. (cr) ©David Young-Wolff/PhotoEdit. (br) ©HMCo./Jade Albert. **R18** (cl) New Noon/Panoramic Images. (bl) ©Reuters/CORBIS. (cr) ©Allan Davey/Masterfile. (br) ©Paul Colangelo/CORBIS. **R19** (tr) ©Roman Soumar/CORBIS. (cl) ©Bettmann/CORBIS. (c) ©Maroon/Folio, Inc. (cr) ©Raymond Gehman/CORBIS. (br) ©Keith Wood/CORBIS. **R20** (cl) ©AGStockUSA, Inc./Alamy. (tr) Shelby County Circuit Court Judges. (cr) ©Steve Dunwell/Getty Images. (cr) Thomas Winz/Panoramic Images. (br) ©Dave G. Houser/CORBIS. (br) ©Michael Newman/PhotoEdit. **R21** (bl) ©Scott Wintrow/Getty Images. (br) ©PictureNet Corporation/Alamy. **R22** (tl) ©Bettmann/CORBIS. (cl) ©Arthur Tilley/Taxi/Getty Images. (bl) ©HMCo./Ken Karp. (tr) AP / Wide World Photos. (cr) ©Charles Gupton/CORBIS. **R23** (tl) ©Mark Heifner/Pan Stock/PictureQuest. (cl) ©HMCo./Angela Coppola. (bl) Scenics of America/PhotoLink. (r) ©CORBIS. (cr) ©Lee Snider/CORBIS. (cl) Jim Wark/AirPhoto. (br) Dan Gair Photographic/Index Stock/PictureQuest. **R24** (tl) ©Stephen Schauer/Stone/Getty Images. (tr) ©HP Merten/Zefa/Masterfile. (cl) ©Jim Craigmyle/CORBIS. (c) ©Bob Thomas/Stone/Getty Images. (cr) ©Imagestate-Pictor/PictureQuest. (br) ©LWA-Dann Tardif/CORBIS. **R25** (tl) ©Paul Barton/CORBIS. (cl) ©Bettmann/CORBIS. (cl) ©Jeffrey Greenberg/Folio, Inc. (bl) ©Joseph Sohm; Visions of America/CORBIS. (tr) © Londie G Padelsky/Panoramic Images. (cl) The Greater Boston Food Bank.